THE FOLIAGE GARDEN

CREATING BEAUTY BEYOND BLOOM

ANGELA OVERY

PHOTOGRAPHS BY ROB PROCTOR

ILLUSTRATIONS BY ANGELA OVERY
AND BARBARA GREGG

FOREWORD BY CHRISTOPHER WOODS

HARMONY BOOKS

NEW YORK

A RUNNING HEADS BOOK

Copyright © 1993 by Quarto Inc.

Published by Harmony Books, 201 East 50th Street,
New York, New York 10022.
Member of the Crown Publishing Group.

HARMONY and colophon are trademarks of Crown Publishers, Inc.

Library of Congress Cataloging-in-Publication Data
Overy, Angela.
The foliage garden : creating beauty beyond bloom / Angela Overy ;
photographs by Rob Proctor ; illustrations by Barbara Gregg ;
foreword by Christopher Woods.—1st ed.
p.   cm.
"A Running Heads book"—Verso t.p.
Includes bibliographical references and index.
ISBN 0-517-59173-1
1. Foliage plants.   2. Gardens—Design.   3. Foliage plants—
Pictorial works.   4. Gardens—Design—Pictorial works.
I. Proctor, Rob.   II. Title.
SB431.O94   1993
635.9'75—dc20   92-26930
CIP

THE FOLIAGE GARDEN
A Running Heads book,
Quarto Inc., The Old Brewery,
6 Blundell Street, London N7 9BH

Creative Director: Linda Winters
Senior Editor: Thomas G. Fiffer
Designer: Jan Melchior
Managing Editor: Jill Hamilton
Production Associate: Belinda Hellinger

Illustrations by Barbara Gregg

Typeset by A&S Graphics Inc.

Color separations by Vimnice Printing Press Co., Ltd.
Printed and bound in Hong Kong by
Leefung–Asco Printers Limited

ISBN 517-59173-1

1   3   5   7   9   10   8   6   4   2

FIRST EDITION

For Richard,

Charles and Alexandra—

the new generation

I should like to inflame the whole world
with my taste for gardening.
There is no virtue that I do not attribute
to the man who lives to project
and execute gardens.

Prince Charles
Joseph De Ligne,
1735–1814

CONTENTS

I am fortunate both to live and work in a garden. I am able to look out of my office window to a sight of great beauty. What I see is foliage. Yes, my eye may be caught by the scarlet roses in one corner, or the pale blue hydrangea just beginning to bloom, but it is the foliage that makes my eye linger over the landscape. I look at the trees and admire their form, but it is the patterns of their leaves that grab my attention. The tall American ash by my window has a coarse frame, but the leaves trace a delicate finery against the sky. The blue spruce in the distance, surrounded by a summer lawn, is a candle of color, almost electric in its vibrancy. Perhaps the greatest foliage effect is a finely cut lawn, crisp against the wild profusion of shrubs and herbaceous perennials. ✑ Underneath the elegantly tapered leaves of a bottlebrush buckeye is the fat, blue presence of a hosta. The hostas are the carnival plants of the foliage world, striped and whorled, puckered and curled. Seemingly escorted by the hosta are the delicate fronds of a maidenhair fern with its fluttering, fan-shaped leaves while its black stems are echoed by the dark purple of a mass of Labrador violets. Ferns are serene, leafy vegetables, graceful but strong. They are underused in the garden, often being relegated to a dark, dry place. But their lacy appearance balances more clumsy plants, holding textural unity together with their quiet intensity. ✑ While designing with foliage may have passed many of us by, foliage has not forgotten us. It stands there waiting for us to discover the famous harmony of leaves. While the color wheel spins merrily on, it is the shape, the texture and the fragrance of leaves that should demand our attention. When we plant a tree, mix shrubs and perennials or make a meadow, it is the foliage and its effect that is longer lasting than the bright ephemera of flowers. It is the sound of leaves in the wind that excites us. "Wind is in the cane, Come along. Cane leaves swaying rusty with talk. Scratching choruses above the guinea's squawk. Wind is in the cane. Come along" (Jean Toomer 1894–1967). ✑ It is the gothic grace of the dark needles of the Nordmann fir, and the scalloped shells of false Hinoki cypress. It is the combination of conical and globular, egg-shapped, spoon-shaped and kidney-shaped. It is the winged and acute, the orbicular and the obtuse. It is the sharp spears of irises reflected in water, and the pearly silver of artemisia balancing the quiet riot of rose blossoms. It is the lisp of willow leaves trailing in a stream, and the tiny spoons of lemon thyme scenting the air when crushed underfoot. It is the celery foliage in a Bloody Mary, and the curled leaves of a Cuban cigar. It is the palm fronds waving over the holiday encampment, and the new mown hay in a golden field. ✑ This splendid book is a long overdue addition to the library of American garden writing. Alexander Pope wrote, "Words are like leaves: and where they most abound, much fruit of sense beneath is rarely found." Yet there are words, leaves and much good sense in these pages.

Christopher Woods ، Wayne, Pennsylvania

Introduction

Foliage encompasses the vast quantity of fascinatingly sized, shaped, textured and colored leaves that form the main theme of a garden. Flowers are an essential element of both plant and garden, but they are the reproductive portions of plants, and, as with humans, reproduction occupies only one stage of a plant's life cycle. By selecting plants for their handsome foliage, gardeners can compose a colorful classical or contemporary garden and enjoy the subtle power of the leafy palette.

Observing a plant's natural habit and preferences and understanding its essential requirements comprise the foundation of all gardening. The first three chapters in this book explain the functions of leaves, how they grow and how gardeners can help maximize the potential of each plant. Subsequent chapters explore and illustrate the whole range of colored foliage. Blue fescues, bright yellow lamiums, bronze castor beans, velvety red coleus and pale turquoise artemisias are but a few of the richly colored plants that are readily available. In addition, there are beautiful variegated foliage plants that grow with green and white stripes, speckles and patterns, and sometimes unexpected shades of pink and burgundy. Many of these plants are new hybrids or introductions from the tropics. Today's gardener is mingling and merging all the colors and patterns of these leaves with foliage of different sizes, from minute thymes to giant inulas, and different textures ranging from lacy ferns to glossy gingers and wrinkly ballotas. The result is new gardens with sophisticated form and studied shape. The savvy gardener understands that foliage is a critical design element in the architecture of the garden.

For about four hundred years gardeners have been growing an increasingly eclectic selection of plants around their dwellings. Now with many people travelling, and television airing hundreds of nature programs, gardeners are more aware than ever of the vast number of plants available. The temptation to try to make a miniature rainforest, minimalist desert or piece of Olde England is nearly irresistible.

The heart of this book leads the gardener through a variety of gardening styles, and helps him or her make appropriate foliage choices. Chapter Four explores the many possibilities for creating leafy bowers and wild woodlands with underplantings. The urban gardener is rediscovering formal gardens and sculptured foliage plants. Crisp patterns of green and varying textures are appearing in traditional topiary, hedges and espaliered trees to create new gardens as structured as a medieval Gregorian chant. Few foliage plants are as reliable, hardy and showy as ferns. Chapter Four features both classic and little-known varieties, including the ethereal and old-fashioned maidenhair fern, the fragrant hay-scented fern and the hairy-fronded cinnamon fern. There are also suggestions for dappled shade gardens and damp and dry shaded borders in the shadow of buildings.

Water gardens have received enthusiastic attention of late, and Chapter Five presents suggestions for foliage plants that grow in and around water. These include giant gunneras, water lilies and ornamental rhubarbs. Depending on design preferences, gardeners may opt for a formal pool surrounded by plantings of fountain grass bamboo and arum lilies, or a natural lake with oozing banks of candelabra primulas, pickerel weed and marsh marigolds.

While we tend to think of ground covers as low-maintenance alternatives to lawns, they can be used to great effect in beds and borders. Chapter Six outlines the possibilities for designing with these plants and forming carpets of intriguingly patterned and colored foliage. Ornamental grasses are generating interest for accent plantings or to evoke a meadow or prairie feeling.

With many parts of the world becoming conscious of a water shortage, drought-resistant plants are also playing an important role in gardens. Many plants with grey and silver foliage thrive in full sun with little moisture. Chapter Seven features distinctive silver and glaucous plants, and explains how to combine them with bright flowers for an elegant Mediterranean mood or a softly bleached desert scene. A number of conifers with sparkling yellow foliage will gleam in a sunny garden. Deciduous trees with yellowish green foliage need more water but are particularly pretty and practical in darker gardens. These include the heart-shaped leafed catalpa and the ancient ginkgo tree. Combined with cream and butter-colored variegated foliage and yellow underplantings, they can be the base of a truly golden garden.

The tropical wet look is the subject of Chapter Eight, which offers a plan for turning a small part of a northern garden into a virtual equatorial paradise. Dripping datura vines, spikes of palm-like phormiums and shiny-leafed fatsia are a few of the plants that can contribute to this illusion.

Planning to decorate a house's exterior with plants can be as fun and challenging as decorating the interior. In Chapter Nine, foliage climbs walls, graces terraces and spills out of pots on patios. Herbs and vegetables have historically been separated from the rest of the garden, but as gardens shrink and gardeners begin to enjoy the delightful range of textured, scented and multicolored leaves, these domestic treasures, such as clary sage and fennel, join the borders.

Chapter Ten pulls everything together. Finding locations around the world with similar climates, temperatures and altitudes to one's own garden is helpful in the selection of appropriate plants. Suggestions are offered for gathering plants together in a harmonious collection that will excite but not overwhelm, and enhance rather than detract from the earth's natural resources.

Grand traditions of the use of foliage in gardening are alive everywhere. This book focuses on some of the areas and themes that are creating contemporary gardens. Attention to the details of foliage and its shape and texture can become an element of many different gardens with diverse moods. For instance, the small sword shapes of Japanese blood grass or the exquisite outline of a cutleaf maple, typical of a Japanese garden, can look equally at home in a contemporary American garden.

Many European countries have also contributed to garden composition. Italian water gardens, fountains and use of statuary have had a great influence, and the garden at Versailles, France, with its elegant, formal layout and use of sculptural foliage and potted citrus trees, has probably been copied and interpreted more than any other garden in the world. Holland is, and always has been, a leader in the growing and introduction of new bulbs and plants, and many mature English gardens are of great historical interest. English gardeners have been designing with trees, shrubs and perennial plants, and have understood the importance of leaves, their colors and shapes, for centuries.

The vast continents of North America and Australia, with their many climatic zones, offer their own versions of gardens, from cool misty green foliage havens in Vancouver to lovely grey foliage themes in Sydney. Now, innovative and elegant foliage gardens can be admired in Sao Paulo, Brazil, Singapore and Frankfurt, and plant experts from Scandinavia to Turkey offer much interesting advice.

With space, leisure time and gardening help limited, today's gardeners are renewing their interest in plants with fine foliage that will remain attractive for most of the year and require less attention. Awareness of a plant's shape and texture is becoming as important as knowing its flower's color. A deeper understanding of plants' basic requirements is leading many gardeners to select plants confidently that will thrive in their microclimate without feeling the need to create a traditional picture-book garden with plants that may be inappropriate. There is no need to plant petunias and marigolds when a group of perennial penstemons and euphorbias might be longer lasting, hardier and just as attractive.

Gardeners are also becoming more conscious of the environment and how dependent we are on the delicate balance of plants and people. Some gardeners are pursuing their own back-to-nature movement, encouraging parts of their property to revert to wild woodland, bog, grassy meadow or primeval prairie. Chapters in this book address using foliage plants close to the house, around the garden and as linkages to these more natural areas of the property. Even the smallest city garden can become an oasis of native plants.

The blending of horticultural relationships is both increasingly complicated and fascinating. Scientific research and breeding provides new hybrids and variations each season. The global exchange of plants is united by the common design themes of order and disorder, line and curve. The role of foliage in the garden will expand as we strive to make sanctuaries and showpieces that are harmonious reflections of the human spirit.

Chapter One

All
About
Leaves

Not a tree, a plant, a leaf,
a blossom, but contains a folio volume.
We may read, and read and read again,
and still find something new.

James Hurdis, 1763–1801

Felt-like silver edges, the
leaves of wooly MULLEIN
(VERBASCUM THAPSUS),
opposite, complemented
by GOLDENWEED
(HAPLOPAPPUS SPINULOSUS).

On the left overleaf,
PIGSQUEAK (BERGENIA
CORDIFOLIA) takes on rosy
autumnal tints. On the right
overleaf, PETASITES
JAPONICUS thrives in moist
shade.

Everyone knows there are billions of leaves in the world, thousands of different kinds, and that they get on quietly with whatever they do. Quite what they do, and whether it matters, is for most of us a mystery. Gardeners are different. Having a rudimentary knowledge of how leaves work, and the reasons for their shapes, sizes and textures, makes a good deal of other garden wisdom fall into place. Unless one is a botanist, the physics, chemistry, and some of the terminology can be a bit daunting, but this is far outweighed by the captivating facts.

On a worldwide basis leaves exchange gases that affect our environment; they manufacture chemicals; they are part of the food chain; they are, in turn, homes, fertilizer, shelter and shade. Unlike animals, plants are self-sufficient. Most animals move around, hunt for food, shelter and a mate, and travel to escape from predators and inhospitable temperatures. Plants have evolved to perform all the same functions while staying in place. Nearly all of the adaptations and variety seen in plants result from this need to grow, reproduce and pass on the genes to the next generation.

Humans may think of leaves as commodities to be harvested or grown in gardens and admired. For plants, however, the primary functions of leaves are photosynthesis, transpiration and the construction of substances like cellulose, starches, fats and proteins. Some leaves have auxiliary jobs such as capturing and digesting insects and other food where the soils do not provide sufficient nutrients, and some act as roots and absorb water, but these differ from the norm.

Plants need water, light, minerals and gases. Water, and substances dissolved in it, are absorbed through a plant's roots and move up the stem and into the foliage by a series of successive steps. Because this process defies gravity, it requires some explanation. Simply put, water moves to equalize the concentration of salts stored in the plant with those stored in the soil. Since the soil salt concentration is weaker, water flows from the soil into the root cells until the amount of salt relative to water in the plant equals the amount in the soil. This process is called osmosis. The water then rises through a system of fine tubes to the top of the plant, from the smallest flower to the tallest redwood tree. These amazing tubes prevent the solution from flowing back down in the soil and regulate the flow of rising water so the leaves do not burst. The average herbaceous plant is approximately 95 percent water; the precise amount varies according to conditions such as the time of day and year and the temperature.

When water is drawn up through the stem and out to the foliage, the sun's heat vaporizes the water, which then escapes the leaves through millions of minute pores called stomata. This is part of a breathing cycle called transpiration. Considering how heavy the water being transported up the trunk of a large tree might be gives one an idea of the strength of the pull of osmosis and transpiration. In most plant species 98 percent of the water entering the roots emerges from the leaves as water vapor, an astonishing figure. Scientists estimate that on a summer day up to fifty-eight gallons of water an hour escape from a midsized silver maple tree. An acre of temperate forest might produce as much as eight thousand gallons per day. This water vapor affects human activity, in cities and especially in the garden. Large numbers of plants and trees may lower the summer temperature, increase the humidity and oxygen available and improve the air quality.

Multicolored *Houttuynia cordata* 'Chameleon', which has a reputation for invasiveness in moist soils, is constrained here in a half-barrel aquatic garden with Water Lettuce (*Pistia stratiotes*) and Water Hyacinths (*Eichhornia crassipes*).

Knowledge of the plant plumbing system enables the gardener to help plants thrive. Cells full of water are turgid and crisp. Leaves that lack moisture wilt. Too much salt in the soil can reverse the osmotic process and cause the leaves to wilt even if they have plenty of water. Although the leaves of oceanside plants are specially adapted to store large salt concentrations, most plants will not compensate well for an excess of salts in the soil.

During the day, when plants are in leaf, another activity called photosynthesis occurs. Energy, in the form of light from the sun, carbon dioxide from the air, and water drawn up from the roots, combines in a chemical process to form food, which is stored in the leaves, and oxygen is given off through the stomata. Chlorophyll, the green pigment in leaves and stems, facilitates photosynthesis. While animals inhale oxygen and exhale carbon dioxide, the reverse occurs in plants. This exchange of gases helps maintain the earth's atmosphere for our survival. As long as twentieth-century civilization continues to produce an excess of carbon dioxide and consume the forests that help to absorb it, the balance of these gases will be in jeopardy.

Plants have evolved to survive while stationary in a number of intriguing ways. When plants have sustained an injury from animals or insects or have been torn by the wind, they can seal off the affected area or send out lateral shoots to replace lost leaves. But holes or rips in leaves will not grow back together. To deter animals from causing damage, some plants grow thorns (which are actually modified branches); some have spines (which are variously modified leaves or stipules); and others, such as the rose, grow prickles, which are often recurved in traditional military fashion to prevent a foe from advancing toward the plant's reproductive parts. Some foliage and stems are covered with thick or stiff hairs that small animals find difficult to digest.

Lithops and a few South African succulents employ camouflage as a defense: the stone-like plants disappear in a rocky landscape. Other plants wield a foul odor as their weapon, while an unappealing taste protects others. Gardeners are familiar with two results of plant attack—skin rashes and blisters—sometimes caused by such plants as euphorbias and giant cowsnip, *Heracleum mantegazzianum*. A number of plants are more subtle and simply accumulate sufficient minerals from the soil to make themselves toxic if devoured. Being too tasty is a disadvantage. Ingesting leaves of the widely grown houseplant *Dieffenbachia*, whose common name is dumb cane, can cause respiratory problems and loss of speech. A few of the familiar garden plants grown in Britain and North America possessing fine but poisonous foliage are the datura, hydrangea, iris, *Kalmia latifolia* and rhododendron species. Even the foliage of such seemingly innocuous favorites as the sweet pea and tomato are poisonous.

Plants not only have to defend themselves, but also must compete against each other to procreate successfully. To ensure access to the most light and air, and to find a niche in which they can survive, leaves have developed with an infinite variety of sizes, shapes and margins, with differing venation, and with many arrangements about their stems. The drawing on page 21 displays the main parts of a simple leaf. Most deciduous leaves have a thin, flat blade, open to catch the most light. Many leaves also have a stalk, or petiole, which provides flexibility in the wind or during heavy rain and keeps the leaf from breaking off. The petiole also helps to distribute the foliage along the stem

The spiny texture of *CIRSIUM SPINOSISSIMUM* contrasts effectively with *STACHYS COCCINEA* and rocks.

to provide the greatest amount of light and air circulation to each leaf. Some petioles even orient their leaf toward the light. Sessile leaves have no petiole; they emerge directly from the stem, as in a veratrum. In perfoliate leaves the stem appears to pierce right through the leaf, as it does in a trillium.

Stipules are small, modified branches that sometimes grow in pairs at the base of the leaf petiole. They often look like tiny, twin leaflets. Between the stem and the leaf (see drawing) is an axillary bud. If a plant's stem tips are damaged by adverse weather or predators, or pruned by gardeners, this bud may awake from dormancy and grow into a whole new branch. Each branch of a plant or tree has the ability to grow more branches, but most of these remain in reserve for emergencies (as any gardener who has tried to eliminate a pesky shrub will attest). Once the stem tips, called meristems, have flowered, they usually will not revert to leaf making.

Flowers are actually modified leaves. Bracts are leaves, too, surrounding an inflorescence that gives the appearance of a flower, as in *Euphorbia marginata* or a Christmas poinsettia. Spathes, such as that of the arum lily, are also another form of leaf.

Leaf blades grow in a host of shapes that supply the gardener with visual clues to a plant's identity and delight the artist with surprising variations. A drawing (see page 20) best shows some of the configurations, which have been divided into groups and termed by botanists. It is thought that no two leaves on earth are identical, making the actual variety of leaves infinite. Science has not yet ascertained why so many different leaf shapes have evolved. Some have an obvious advantage, such as a grooved main vein and a sharp point at the tip that directs rain down to the plant roots. The

reasons for other adaptations are not clear.

A single leaf growing alone on a stem, such as an oak leaf, is termed a simple leaf. Other leaves may look simple but are actually compound, with a number of leaflets attached to the petiole. They may be double or even triple compound, with increasingly smaller leaflets that result in a lighter, airy leaf. This creates less shade for the leaves beneath than a large, simple leaf and allows more air to circulate.

Environmental extremes dictate the size of leaves. In the Arctic and above the timberline, where the growing season is as short as six weeks, plants hug the earth in low mounds for protection from winds, heavy snow and exaggerated temperature changes. Whole plants tend to be miniature, and leaves are small and often tough and leathery.

In hot, dry climates, leaf size is dictated by the urge to expose a minimum of surface to the sun. These leaves tend to be small and narrow. For example, cactus leaves may become modified to spines, while the stem swells to take over the traditional leaf role and facilitate storage. The pleated surface of a barrel-shaped cactus enables it to expand and contract, while the corrugations provide some shade and a conduit for scarce rain drops. Many succulents that flourish in a hot climate also have thick, waxy leaves that store moisture.

Leaves in more temperate climates have a greater variety of shapes and sizes. They tend to be larger, and the blades more flat and translucent, to take advantage of sunlight. In partial or dappled shade, leaves are generally larger than in the sunny border, with the biggest leaves found in damp locations. The most colossal and prolific foliage, however, is reserved for the warmest and wettest areas, where a wide variety of tropical and subtropical plants abound.

The edges of leaves, called leaf margins, are another characteristic of leaf shape. Margins are basically smooth, toothed or lobed. Toothed margins may be serrated in a number of ways: sharply with regular indentations, softly with rounded serrations, doubly serrated, divided or deeply divided and many permutations in between. Some leaf margins enhance the three-dimensional, irregular shape of the leaf with edges that undulate gently or ruffle in sinuous curves. Other margins are spined, as in some hollies, and yet others are fringed with hairs. A selection of these appears in the drawing on page 20.

The veins on leaves serve as part of the plant's vascular system. They connect the roots, stem or trunk with the foliage, conducting food and water to and from the various cells. Plants such as grasses, bamboos, lilies and irises have "parallel veins" along their leaves, although these veins do come to a point at the tip. On other plants, the leaves may have palmately arranged veins spread out in a fan shape from the petiole, as does lady's-mantle, *Alchemilla mollis,* or be pinnately venated with a central main rib and smaller veins branching out from either side. Both of these patterns have increasingly small veins forming a fine net over the plant's epidermis, and an elaborate distribution system that resembles the small blood vessels in our own skin.

Not only do countless combinations of leaf shapes and margins exist throughout the world, but leaves are also arranged in different ways along the stem, as shown on page 21. It has not been determined why these arrangements differ and whether some are more effective than others. But it is clear that each arrangement does offer leaves a piece of the action by giving them access to light. Leaves may grow in pairs along the stem opposite each other, or they may be spaced alternately. When a bunch of leaves radiates from one point on a stem, they are whorled, as in martagon lilies. Basal leaves are grouped at ground level, sometimes loosely arranged like sea lavender, *Limonium latifolium,* sometimes in exquisite rosettes.

In full, bright sun, plant stems are apt to be short and the leaves closely spaced. In shadier areas the stems of sun-loving plants are elongated, the leaves spaced farther apart as the stem tips reach toward the light. Shade-loving plants fortunate enough to grow in shade do not have such limitations and can grow as broad, tall or leafy as space permits.

Page 21 displays a simple diagram of a cross section of a deciduous leaf. The outermost layer or cuticle is the leaf's first line of defense against invasions by molds, insects or too much sunlight. Between the epidermis layers is an arrangement of cells where complex chemical reactions take place. On the undersides of most leaves, for protection from weather and dust, are thousands of stomata, or pores. In some leaf spears, such as iris, stomata are on both sides, as there is no "underside." Each minute aperture is flanked by a pair of guard cells that open and close the hole according to the plant's needs. Stomata are open during normal day temperatures but will close in very hot sun. A plant may wilt on a hot day even if the soil is damp, but will become erect again during cooler evening hours. Most stomata close at night when photosynthesis ceases or when the soil is too dry, the weather is too hot or winds are too strong. At these times, transpiration slows or stops altogether, because conserving water becomes the plant's first priority. Desert plants adapt to the

SOME EXAMPLES OF LEAF SHAPES, MARGINS AND VENATION

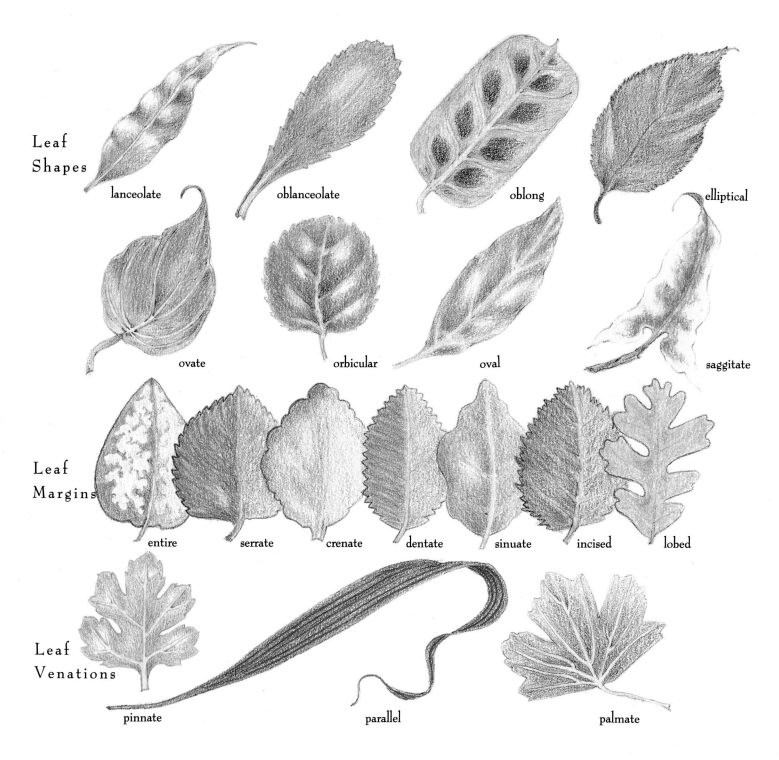

Leaf Shapes

lanceolate

oblanceolate

oblong

elliptical

ovate

orbicular

oval

saggitate

Leaf Margins

entire

serrate

crenate

dentate

sinuate

incised

lobed

Leaf Venations

pinnate

parallel

palmate

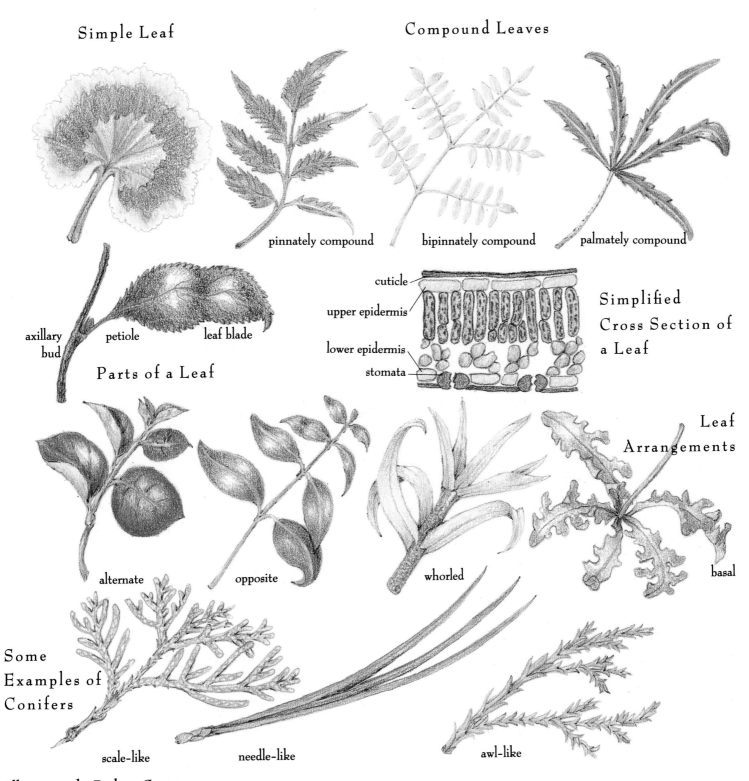

Simple Leaf

Compound Leaves

pinnately compound

bipinnately compound

palmately compound

Parts of a Leaf

axillary bud

petiole

leaf blade

cuticle

upper epidermis

lower epidermis

stomata

Simplified Cross Section of a Leaf

Leaf Arrangements

alternate

opposite

whorled

basal

Some Examples of Conifers

scale-like

needle-like

awl-like

Illustration by Barbara Gregg

The delicate fronds of INTERMEDIATE FERN (*DRYOPTERIS INTERMEDIA,*) opposite above, belie a strong constitution.

Dew-catching LADY'S MANTLE (*ALCHEMILLA MOLLIS*), opposite below, mingles with a variegated form of *EUONYMUS FORTUNEI.*

heat by opening their stomata at night, thereby preventing too much evaporation.

Leaves require a period of adjustment when plants that have been nurtured in greenhouses or indoors are taken outside for spring planting. The stomata may need at least a week to adapt to the altered light and temperature. These plants should be protected or left in the shade on a terrace for a while. Similarly, when plants are brought indoors in the autumn, chemical changes and changes in the stomata must take place for the plant to survive. Also, plants do not like to be jiggled. Take care when transporting them not to shake them or expose them to harsh, drying winds.

Deciduous plants have leaves that fall off in the winter, in contrast to evergreens, whose leaves may last several years and drop off gradually. Most conifers—trees that bear cones—are evergreen, but some, such as larch, lose their needles in winter. Evergreen is a broad term. There are many nonconifer evergreens, such as helianthemum, and some plants are evergreen only in mild winters.

Because leaves of conifers are adapted to survive through all four seasons, the leaves of pines, spruces, firs and junipers are not as broad and flat as those of deciduous trees. Their minimum surface probably helps them endure climatic extremes. The so-called needles of an adult pine are enclosed in a fascicle—a bundle of from one to five leaves. Spruce leaves are square in cross section, stiff and sharply pointed, and are spirally arranged in peg-like projections along the twig. When the leaves finally drop off after seven to ten years, these projections remain, giving the spruce twig a rough texture. Firs also have long-lived, spirally arranged single leaves. Their needles are flexible, however, and appear blunt and flat in cross

section. When fir needles drop off, the twig is left smooth with only small scars. Juniper leaves tend to be very small, awl- or scale-shaped, and they lie flat and neatly against the twig.

Perhaps more than any other aspect, the texture of foliage attracts us to certain plants. Marsh marigolds, such as *Caltha polypetala,* bask in spring beside a pool, their puckered surfaces reflecting facets of sunlight. In summer lamb's-ears, *Stachys byzantina,* nestle into the bed, melting the soft-hearted with their appealing fuzziness, only to look like comfortable old grey sweaters with matted woolen leaves in winter. There is a texture for every taste, from sleek grasses to lustrous magnolias to dainty rues.

Textures, however, are just another survival adaptation. Shiny foliage repels rain and permits fast drying. In tropical forests this prevents fungi from growing on the leaf. Deeply grooved leaves, such as *Hosta fortunei* 'Marginato-alba', have increased surface area and create a dramatic pattern of light and shade. Pleated, puckered, folded and fringed—these terms sound like dress-making instructions but aptly describe a few of the textures that can be stitched into a garden.

There are at least nine botanical terms for describing hairy plants: downy, hirsute, hoary, pilose, villose, pubescent, tomentose, ciliate and chrysocoma. Apart from being good for crossword puzzles, they accurately portray the range of wooliness in the plant world. Most hairs are white, often giving a greyish or silvery cast to the leaves, but there are many colored hairs such as the long, brown hair-like scales on the fiddlehead of some ferns, and purple hairs on some begonia leaves. Some hairs are pubescent, soft and short, while others are like a silky beard. Epidermal hair slows

water evaporation and reflects harsh sunlight from the leaf. The downiest foliage is found in climates with the most sun and at higher altitudes.

A different, contrasting texture that combats the sun by reflecting light and storing moisture is found in the fleshy foliage group. Glabrous succulents, such as sedums and ice plants, have an attractive, waxy texture much sought after in rock gardens and as ground covers. Many leaves sport different textures on their upper and lower surfaces that provide added interest in the garden. For instance, some smooth, dark green rhododendron leaves reverse to a short, brown felt underneath. Soil can be a determining factor in a plant's texture. In poor, sandy soil foliage may be tough and coriaceous, while the same type of plant in good loamy soil may flourish luxuriously.

The texture of leaves conjures up moods and memories. Leaves with spiked margins, such as those of some mahonias, evoke a certain martial fierceness. The huge leaves of the common fig, *Ficus carica,* bring to mind Adam and Eve, and the fairylike, bright green leaves of the emerging larch, which arrive in spring, remind me of my childhood in the English countryside and a house full of leaves and flowers. The scabious texture of palms, which rustle and scratch each other in the moonlight, makes me think of warm holidays by the sea, and I can never see a softly textured, mossy bank without visualizing Titania and Bottom's hilarious love scene in a *Midsummer Night's Dream.*

Whether we hanker after the tidy, elegant texture of clipped boxwood, or fancy flitting into a feathery glade of ferns, the texture of foliage can be the key to designing a classic garden for the coming century.

Chapter Two

The Foliage Palette

Infinite numbers, delicacies, smells,

With hues on hues expression cannot paint,

The breath of Nature and her endless bloom.

James Thomson, 1700–1748
The Seasons

An outstretched limb of blue ATLAS CEDAR (*CEDRUS ATLANTICA* 'GLAUCA') at the Scott Arboretum, opposite, underscores dark-leaved HYACINTH BEAN (*DOLICHOS LABLAB,* now *DIPOGON LABLAB*), BLUE AVENA GRASS (*HELICTOTRICHON SEMPERVIRENS*).

On the left overleaf, *COREOPSIS VERTICILLATA* 'MOONBEAM' shines over *PULMONARIA SACCHARATA* 'MRS. MOON'. On the right overleaf, *HEDERA COLCHICA* 'SULPHUR HEART' is an outstanding variegated ivy.

If asked to draw a leaf, the average person would sketch a simple blade, add a stem and color it green. Many people are attuned to thinking of leaves as a primary source of color only during autumn. With some judicious planning, however, garden foliage can be as exhilarating as a rainbow and have just as many hues. Two or three plants of each color of the spectrum highlight the vast array of colored foliage.

More people prefer blue than any other color, and a range of blue foliage is an important element in a creative garden. *Festuca caesia,* also recognized as *Festuca ovina glauca,* is the finest of a series of blue fescue grasses, which are a soft Cape Cod blue. The slim, elegant leaves are tightly bunched, so they stand up in a lively manner. In summer, they turn almost turquoise, providing a cool contrast at the front of a vividly colored bed. In a flower bed next to a white-capped ocean, mounds of blue fescue would look crisp and nautical teamed with frothy white flowers. Even in winter when dead cream-colored leaves mingle with the blue, it has a strangely pleasing appearance of weaving sea and sand.

Colorado blue spruce, *Picea pungens,* is a handsome specimen tree with several blue cultivars. It maintains its icy blue foliage year-round, is hardy in bitter cold and looks attractive draped in snow or with icicles dripping from its small, tight, beige cones, conjuring up visions of the Snow Queen in *The Nutcracker* in a blue tutu covered with silver sequins.

For a glabrous, broad-leafed texture, *Hosta tardiflora* 'Hadspen Blue' is refreshing as a waterfall, its blue blades cascading in cool, sapphire layers. This hosta's smooth leaf margins, sleek surface and glacial grey-blue color have a calming effect in a garden. As an alternative, *H. sieboldiana*

'Elegans' has great blue-green leaves with a rippling stream texture and wild, sinuous margins. The leaves of blue hostas are actually a soft green with a waxy bloom as delicate as the finish on antique furniture. Care should be taken to prevent hail, lawn mowers and even slugs from damaging their pristine surface.

There is such an array of purple foliage that it would be possible to have a whole purple garden— a nightmare well suited to Dracula's castle on the Danube. Because most purple foliage is dark and dramatic, it can overwhelm neighboring plants, but it can be a fine foil for pale pink and blue flowers, and for more delicate foliage. A purple-leafed canna, such as *Canna indica* 'Egandale', provides monstrous drama, particularly when the scarlet blooms appear late in summer. In a large masculine garden this performance can be splendid. Some plants are simply more appealing than others, and it is hard to specify why. *Cotinus coggygria* 'Royal Purple', a charming, deciduous shrub with orbicular leaves, is in this category. 'Royal Purple' and 'Notcutt's Variety' both have rich, purple foliage that turns a stunning red in autumn. To create a purple undergrowth there are two forms of ajuga that enjoy shade and flower readily in dappled sunshine. *Ajuga reptans* 'Atropurpurea' has a purplish brown glossy foliage, while 'Burgundy Glow' sports magenta and pink leaves with a startling cream margin.

Although scarlet foliage is usually associated with autumn in temperate climates, there are many plants that show red and even bright pink foliage during spring and summer. One of the prettiest is *Pieris,* an evergreen shrub. *Pieris formosa* 'Forrestii' and 'Forest Flame' are two members of this species that have white flowers and bottle green, lance-shaped leaves. The young leaves are brilliant red,

Valued by gardeners for their summer flowers, CRANESBILLS, such as *GERANIUM* X *CANTABRIGIENSE*, put on a splendid late-season foliage display.

creating a Christmas-in-May color scheme that gradually fades to summery peach and salmon shades. With its superglossy foliage and lipstick coloring, this plant could have been invented by a fashion magazine as a prop for the young executive on her way up. Pieris flourish best in acidic soil. *Photinia* 'Red Robin', commonly called red tip bush,

also has scarlet new growth; millions of visitors to Williamsburg have admired the photinia each spring, glowing against the verdant Virginian forests and white-flowered magnolias.

Dragon's blood is a fanciful name for a down-to-earth little *Sedum spurium*. Dark green whorled foliage becomes blood red in autumn and retains

wall. The leaves of this deciduous shrub are half green, with the apex a bright shrimp pink. The young foliage of many plants is a different color and texture. New leaves may be a pink or reddish color, particularly in tropical areas.

The next colors in the rainbow palette are yellow and orange. Although these colors are associated with autumn, some plants, mostly trees, display sunny colored foliage throughout the summer. Whether they are planted to brighten a dark corner or to blaze away in the sun, their gold tones add luminosity to any color scheme.

Acer japonicum 'Aureum' is a Japanese maple that requires light shade for the foliage to achieve its glorious sunset colors. All through summer the leaves are pale gold; then the center of each leaf turns red with an orange margin, and finally as scarlet as a setting sun. Among the other fine yellow trees, *Robinia pseudoacacia* 'Frisia' is an obvious choice when a small specimen tree with dainty gold foliage is desired, while some experts consider the big, heart-shaped leafed *Catalpa bignonioides* 'Aurea' the most distinctive tree. *Chamaecyparis lawsoniana* 'Lane' is only one of a range of beautiful conifers that retains its bright yellow foliage year-round. On a grey wintery day, it can gleam against a stark landscape.

Naturally there are more greens in the garden palette than any other color, but their astonishing variety and virescent textures make them particularly riveting. There is no juicier lime green than the marsh spurge, *Euphorbia palustris*, no more emerald green than the common curly parsley, no fresher green than the unfurling frond of a fern. The darkest greens, such as camellias, and the palest, such as the soft, woolly greens of *Ballota pseudodictamnus*, are worth planting to add entrancing contrasting shades.

COPPERLEAF (*ACALYPHA WILKESIANA*), gleams like a polished tea kettle.

this color all winter. It forms a thick ground cover rather like a Turkish carpet with patterns of brick red, maroon and dark green—an excellent way to extend a fine interior to a matching patio outdoors. For anyone enamored of pink and green combinations, there is nothing prettier than the foliage of *Actinidia kolomikta* growing against a grey

Gentle beiges and deep browns are not within the rainbow hues but are nonetheless an important part of a garden's design. *Ricinus communis* 'Gibsonii' is an extremely fast-growing, tall annual with great palmately divided leaves in a rich brown shoe-leather color. So much beautiful grey and silver foliage exists that it fills a whole chapter here.

Leaves shimmer in a thousand shades of color, and to compound their sumptuousness, some have variegated patterns as well. Variegated species of plants have been considered an asset in the garden for centuries. Many gardeners have been unable to resist the variegated cultivar of a species and have opted for the cream-margined, or perhaps the blotched green and white variety, of a common plant. A broad range of patinations—including mottled, striped, speckled and zoned—and hues from palest cream to purple add zest to a plant collection.

Different leaf colors derive from the complexities of plant chemistry. Additional chemicals in the foliage are responsible for red or blue tones, and chlorophyll makes leaves appear green. As the quantity of chlorophyll decreases, leaves turn from a pale, lime green to yellow, then to cream and finally to white.

There are a number of causes of variegated foliage. For some leaves variegation is an evolutionary adaptation to light and shade; for instance, shade-loving plants may reduce the area available for photosynthesis by decreasing the area of chlorophyll exposed to sunlight, and appear perhaps a banded green and white. Some plants need to absorb a broader spectrum of colored light; leaves in shades of pink or red help satisfy this requirement. Other variegations have evolved successfully to attract pollinators to a plant. A poinsettia, for example, becomes variegated when

sexually receptive; in other plants pale spots may be caused by air pockets within the blade. Some leaves taste vile, and their distinctive pattern of variegation acts as a warning to herbivores, birds and insects. A few of the marbleized leaf patterns are caused by viral infections; leaf mosaic virus is the most familiar. Some viruses are highly contagious, and care must be taken when pruning variegated trees such as abutilon, fraxinus and sorbus.

Variegation is a broad term for a wide range of different leaf markings, some more attractive than others, and the selection of foliage in a garden is a matter of personal taste. Many plant enthusiasts find striped foliage captivating and use striking color combinations to great effect. Others prefer spotted leaves, such as lungwort, *Pulmonaria saccharata*—named because it appears to be sprinkled with sugar.

When leaves are striped, the different chemicals in them are arranged in orderly segments along the blade. For example, in cream and green combinations a distinct line separates the parts of the leaf with and without chlorophyll. *Yucca filamentosa* 'Bright Edge' is a typical example of longitudinal stripes; it has handsome strap-shaped leaves with yellow margins. Horizontal stripes tend to be blended, however, as in *Miscanthus sinensis* 'Zebrinus', an aptly named grass with green and yellow bands across its narrow blades.

Leaves with variegated margins always attract attention. The graphic quality of solid color and contrasting line can appear lacy at a distance, but on closer inspection the variegation takes on the mood of bold hieroglyphics. In the shade or against a dark background, broad white- or cream-margined leaves can paint a particularly dramatic picture. Many variegated hostas excel in this regard. Occasionally, their foliage is white with

A sharp contrast in leaf form and coloration, left, mark this pairing of PURPLE SAGE (*SALVIA OFFICINALIS* 'PURPUREA') and variegated MEXICAN MINT (*PLECTRANTHUS AMBOINICUS* 'WEDGEWOOD VARIEGATED').

An infusion of maroon serves to distinguish the leaves of diverse plants such as the tropical water lily 'EVELYN RANDIG'.

green margins, as in *Hosta* 'White Cap', but more commonly the center of the leaf is green with a pale margin, as in *Hosta fortunei* 'Marginaro-alba', which should be grown in shade because of a paucity of chlorophyll. In some species the cells in the white part of the leaf grow at a rate different than those in the green parts, which makes the leaves grow distorted and puckered, as in *Hosta undulata* 'Medio-variegata'.

A different pattern of variegation results when there is little or no chlorophyll along the venation of a leaf. These leaves appear a shade of green with contrasting ghostly veins, as illustrated by some coleus and begonias. A tender shrub whose variegation is a conversation piece is *Abutilon pictum* 'Thompsonii'. Its leaves have an abstract checkered design in various shades of pale to midgreen, and they look a great deal like a satellite photograph of rice fields.

Some variegations occur naturally, but most appear in increasingly sophisticated horticultural cultivars, with new strains appearing each year.

Very few can be grown true from seed; most are propagated from cuttings or by division. Generally less hardy than their regular counterparts, variegated plants have smaller leaves, and they are predisposed to be more fragile and sensitive to temperature and moisture levels. Light-colored leaf variegations require at least some shade if they are not to burn, while yellow or gold variegations are more robust—some can be grown in full sun.

One cannot write about variegation without mentioning tricolors—for some gardeners the ultimate joy, while others regard them as the depths of depravity. A few are *Salvia officinalis* 'Tricolor', a common sage whose leaves are grey, cream, pink, red and purple; *Amaranthus tricolor* 'Joseph's-coat'; the *Coleus blumei* group with brilliantly colored foliage; and pelargoniums grown just for their foliage, such as 'Mrs. Henry Cox', who looks handsome isolated in stone pots on a patio. Designing a garden around all these enthralling variations, the gardener can paint a canvas as ethereal as a Monet or as bold as a Mondrian.

Maroon markings on some forms of *AJUGA REPTANS*, such as 'BURGUNDY GLOW', make it a valuable groundcover for difficult, shady areas.

Selections from the Foliage Palette

PURPLE OR BRONZE LEAVES

Atriplex hortensis '**Rubra**'(red orache) Tall annual "weed" for startling contrast in the mixed border.

Perilla frutescens (Chinese basil) Performs in sun or part-shade to contrast with pastel flowers.

Heuchera micrantha '**Palace Purple**' Tiny ivory bells top clumps of bronze-red foliage for underplanting peonies or accenting primroses or poppies.

Ajuga reptans '**Caitlin's Giant**' Crinkled, larger-than-ordinary leaves for banks, edging and tough, shady spots.

Ophiopogon planiscapus **var.** *nigrescens* (monkey grass) Nearly black leaves are a valuable accent with silver or blue foliage at front of groupings.

BLUE LEAVES

Ruta graveolens (rue) Cool and refreshing in mixed border with cream and yellow flowers and variegated grasses.

Hosta sieboldiana '**Elegans**' Best among fine-textured goatsbeard and astilbes.

Glaucium flavum (horned poppy) Honey-yellow flowers are followed by prominent "horned" seed pods over wavy, blue leaves in rock gardens and seaside gardens.

Rosa glauca Single pink flowers enhance unique blue-grey leaves with new growth maroon red for a long season of interest.

Thalictrum speciosissimum (meadow rue) Mid to back of the border perennial with pale yellow flowers emphasizing blue foliage.

The autumn tint of BOSTON IVY (*PARTHENOCISSUS TRICUSPIDATA*) cloaks a stucco wall.

Chapter Three

A Study in Green

It is a truly satisfactory thing to see a garden
well schemed and wisely planted. Well-schemed
are the operative words. Every garden, large or
small, ought to be planned from the outset,
getting its bones, its skeleton, into the shape
that it will preserve all through the year even
after the flowers have faded and died away.

Vita Sackville-West, 1892–1962

GARDEN COMPOSITION

A carefully orchestrated planting at New York's Wave Hill with *SEDUM TELEPHIUM* var. *MAXIMUM* 'ATROPURPUREUM', PEARLY EVERLASTING *(ANAPHALIS TRIPLINERVIS)* and *SALVIA LEUCANTHA*, left, is dominated by a juniper with a cloak of *CLEMATIS VITICELLA*.

On the left overleaf, the cool-colored leaves of PINKS *(DIANTHUS* spp.), *BALLOTA ACETABULOSA* and *ARTEMISIA ABSINTHIUM* 'POWIS CASTLE' surround *SEDUM SPECTABILE* 'AUTUMN JOY' at Chanticleer in Pennsylvania. On the right overleaf, the leaves of INDIAN BLANKET FLOWER *(GAILLARDIA* X *GRANDIFLORA)*, PARTRIDGE FEATHER *(TANACETUM DENSUM* var. *AMANI)* and WILD THYME *(THYMUS SERPYLLUM)* form a trio of shapes and colors.

When I first started to garden around a little rented house, I had three criteria for selecting plants: they had to be cheap, showy and fast growing. Years later, and after lots of mistakes and expert advice, my priorities have changed. When one owns a garden and plans to be there a long time, all sorts of possibilities arise, even planting for future generations. The Georgian planters of arboretums thought this perfectly natural, but at the end of the twentieth century it threatens to appear quaint as the number of families who keep their gardens for a hundred years or more is limited. Today, when marketability of one's home is a primary concern, it is more important than ever to plant a garden for year-round interest and to use the timeless principles of good design. Whether one has a tiny, walled garden, a suburban lot or an estate, the five keys to garden composition are color, size, shape, texture and line.

Although climate and soil quality to a large extent determine the actual selection of plants, the color of the house and the quality of light are major factors. For instance, dark, woodland sites with wood siding call for pale-colored, airily textured foliage; whereas a light-colored stucco house under an open sky is enhanced by more vivid colors and textures.

We cannot demand to have attractive people around us all the time, but there is no reason we shouldn't be surrounded by attractive plants. It is often the subtle aspects that one finds most riveting. Beautiful leaf textures, the layering of a delicately leafed plant over contrasting broad, basal foliage, letting one plant creep above and flower right through another—these are all familiar and happy scenes.

*S*ALVIA *AETHIOPSIS* spreads
its silver rosette.

Planting a garden is a little like stocking a supermarket, where the managers put their best-selling items at eye level. They also stock the top and bottom shelves with tantalizing goods everyone wants, just to keep one looking high and low. In a similar manner interesting tall plants, such as towering grasses or slender conifers, encourage one to look up and admire the foliage delineated against billowing clouds or a clear blue sky. Against the heavens the highest leaves and bare branches take on a Pointillistic quality. Silhouetted on a bright day, backlit by the sunshine, the colors are especially brilliant and translucent. Individual shapes are scarcely discernible in the glistening aura. On a cloudy day, however, the colors and forms are opaque. Cumulus clouds scudding behind a tree and reappearing at the other side have entranced people of all civilizations. At dawn and dusk the exquisite dark details of line and form are highlighted against a pale yellow or fiery colored sky.

A lanky plant can look quite different when viewed from several different perspectives. I remember looking up to appreciate some pampas grass, *Cortaderia selloana,* its creamy plumes shifting in front of a speedwell blue sky, then walking a few paces to see the same beige plumes profiled against swarthy green pines, and finally climbing upstairs and looking out the window to see the same plumes from above, this time traced over an emerald lawn, making a waving circle of cream and green—three very different aspects of the same plant.

Moving down closer to eye level, one sees mostly green foliage layered in front of more foliage. This provides a melange, a tapestry where the changes of color and texture are important so each plant can show to advantage. Here the eye searches for a focus, seeks darks against lights,

HOUSELEEKS (*SEMPERVIVUM* spp.) and thyme colonize a
garden retaining wall.

different forms and shapes to accentuate clarity and depth. Foliage in a garden in this middle range, between two and six feet (0.6–1.8 m) high, commands the most attention because it is the easiest to look at and admire. This is the area where it is possible to select from a huge assortment of garden plants to have the choicest foliage, flowers, fruits and berries just inches from the eye.

Finally there is the foliage at one's feet. Everyone glances down more often than up, if only to see where they are going. But unless one is crawling around weeding or planting, the diminutive plants do not receive the diligent regard of their colleagues at eye level. I have always delighted in lying on the ground trying to observe plants from the perspective of a mouse or an ant. Looking up at a growing crocus or eustoma from underneath is a challenge, and although fascinating, one has to face the fact that most of the time all these plants will be observed from a bird's-eye view—that is, straight down. The intricate patterns formed by basal foliage, tight mounds and rosettes are most clearly observed from above. There is nothing so fresh and exciting as peering down into the tremulous, delicate hues of new growth, and savoring the whorls of emerging leaves and incipient flowers.

The ground-level plants in a garden may form a close carpet of colored foliage, or they may be individual plants seen against bare earth, mulch or rocks. Many mulches are available. Nearly every plant looks its best against small weathered strips of grey aspen wood. Tiny grey leaves might look nondescript lying on tiny bits of grey gravel, but ravishing emerging from round, cream-colored pebbles.

In the interest of economy, I have sometimes

bought an ugly-shaped plant with the vain idea that I could trim it or it would improve. Almost invariably it grew into a larger ungainly plant. This becomes a particular problem if the monstrosity is a tree and a feature of a small garden. Some plants are programmed genetically to grow in fine shapes, however, and it is worth seeking out a fine selection of tall, medium and short plants in good architectural shapes.

Some plants grow in neat mounds without any help from the gardener. When one reads in seed or plant catalogues "forms mounds of foliage," this means the plant will appear naturally clipped. Other plants will naturally form tidy fans, cones, spheres or looser, unstructured shapes. Getting to know the habits of different species is extremely helpful in planning a garden. The aim is to make a sculpture of living shapes, so that if a black-and-white photograph were taken of the garden it would still look interesting. Whether the garden's design has a free form, a controlled Japanese layout or something in between, the individual plant shapes and their positions will play a major part in its appearance and mood.

Along with an attention to different plant heights, varying the textures in a garden adds interest and charm. Combining several textures together in a bed or flower pot is nearly always successful. The airy young foliage of a dewy columbine, budding bleeding heart and adolescent maidenhair fern can snuggle up seductively against one of the masculine rodgersia, or the stout-hearted and leathery *Bergenia cordifolia*. The shifting, long, narrow, strap-shaped leaves of ornamental grasses make the gigantic leaves of ornamental rhubarb, *Rheum palmatum,* look even more imposing and massive. This type of planting of dissimilar textures can be carried out with

PEPPERMINT-SCENTED GERANIUM (*PELARGONIUM TOMENTOSUM*) meets JAPANESE BARBERRY (*BERBERIS THUNBERGII* 'ATROPURPUREA').

foliage of different sizes, colors and shapes. At the front of a flower bed the minute leaves of lemon thyme, *Thymus* X *citriodorus*, arranged jauntily on their miniature bushes, make the small, pleated, round leaves of lady's-mantle, *Alchemilla mollis*, appear positively huge and tropical. It is all a matter of scale, as well as constantly trying to make each plant look its best.

Line is another significant part of garden

The yellow blossoms of *STERNBERGIA CLUSIANA* appear in autumn amidst *STACHYS BYZANTINA* 'HELENE VON STEIN' and HELICHRYSUM PETIOLAIRE 'LIMELIGHT'.

composition. The old masters, such as Velásquez, composed their paintings with consummate skill. They used diagonals, such as an outstretched arm, for emphasis, movement and to direct the eye to their primary subject. The lines of architectural features gave depth. Tall verticals, such as trees or standing men, provided strength and stability to the composition, while in the background horizontal lines conveyed serenity. These same skills can be applied to composing a garden, even one the size of an old master's large canvas.

Many plants have natural horizontal lines such as the pagoda dogwood, *Cornus alternifolia*, a small, deciduous tree with flat tiers of leaves. This tree is especially pretty in spring, when it has alternate layers of cream–colored flowers. A similar effect is produced by *Viburum plicatum* 'Mariesii'. Vertical lines of many heights are provided by fastigiate trees such as columnar Leyland cypress (X *Cupressocyparis leylandii*). Perennials like cimicifuga, ligularia and verbascum make strong, midsized verticals in the bed, while the short, shooting spikes of *Iris pallida* or black-leafed grass, *Ophiopogon planiscapus* var. 'nigrescens', add dashes of life to the base of a garden composition.

Arching branches provide lovely, sweeping lines that give a lyrical quality to the garden. Many grasses will vault gracefully over smaller plants. Not only will *Crocosmia* 'Lucifer' leaves arch elegantly, but its scarlet flowers will also leap forward like a splash of molten lava. Weeping, flowing foliage evokes a languid mood, irresistible beside water. Even in a dry garden the lax look promotes instant torpor, ideal for the gardener with a slightly nervous disposition.

Memories and fantasies influence our most basic urges to create a haven in our gardens. Imagine an immense, old, grey-trunked, green-leafed wisteria climbing over a white Victorian conservatory, the glorious purple inflorescences cascading down the glass and dripping off the edges. Such images can inspire creative uses of weeping and arching leaves.

A sharp change of pace can invigorate the senses, and plants with bold, spiky foliage achieve this successfully. Agave, aloes and yuccas all grow in rosettes of many sizes. With sharp, narrow leaves shooting out in all directions, they are impossible to ignore. In a somnolent glade they offer shock value. In a sunny, flowery and fussy border they provide welcome drama. On a spare, contemporary terrace, they are the best kind of sculpture.

Buying a house with an established garden is exciting for most gardeners. It offers an opportunity to conduct the kind of makeover seen in magazines, where an ugly living room becomes a breathtaking boudoir. When somebody else has spent back-breaking hours weeding, digging and caring for a plant, and their hard-earned money paying for it, the new owner can afford to be dispassionate about relocating or dispensing with it. Redesigning a garden with more character, more height and depth, more texture and more contrast in leaf shapes, sizes and colors, is every gardener's dream.

WEEPING CANADA HEMLOCK (*TSUGA CANADENSIS* 'PENDULA') cascades down boulders in the rock alpine garden at Denver Botanic Gardens.

Foliage as Focus, Backdrop and Screen

Gardeners think of plants as friends, as lovers, as someone to fight with or admire inordinately; but they find it hard to stand back dispassionately and choose plants that are simply useful. Even I admit to being perennially swept off my feet by double, pinkpetalled peonies. Many gardeners tend to be so infatuated with certain flowers that they find it difficult to see that their favorite might be enhanced through association with another plant, or framed by foliage. Well-sited foliage plants can make an enormous difference to the way observers perceive a garden. The subtle use of plants as backdrops, accents, disguises and more can make the difference between a lovely garden and a great one.

Plants without a backdrop are like a stage without scenery. Flowers and actors both look best with the scene set in depth, color and mood. The ideal backdrop is great deep beds with room for fine conifers and deciduous trees, then a selection of handsome shrubs and tall grasses backing a variety of perennials and annuals. Another backdrop might be a row of evergreens, a hedge or an informal grouping of small trees and shrubs. To various extents these will all screen out the sight of neighbors—even if not their voices—act as windbreaks and perhaps create a milder climate within their shelter.

Tall backdrops do not have to take the form of straight lines on three sides of a garden. They can swoop up on the north side to screen an eyesore, curve down on the east to let in early morning sunshine, and be at their lowest on the south, or whatever is necessary. Backdrops can frame a view. However small or limited, the view will be improved if explored between the branches of such splendid trees as the evergreen strawberry tree, *Arbutus unedo*, which is partial to Mediterranean

A curtain of JAPANESE BARBERRY (*BERBERIS THUNBERGII* 'ATROPURPUREA') showcases a chorus of ICELAND POPPIES (*PAPAVER NUDICAULE*) *in a garden in Vail.*

At New York Botanical Gardens, GLOBE AMARANTH (*GOMPHRENA HAAGEANA* 'STRAWBERRY FAIR') glistens in front of AMERICAN ARBORVITAE (*THUJA OCCIDENTALIS* 'ERICOIDES').

climates, or the deciduous Japanese tree lilac, *Syringa reticulata*. One must, however, guard against trees taking over and blocking the view. It is sad to see a house with alluring vistas blocked by overgrown branches.

A foliage backdrop can even have a hole cut in it to create interest and entice the eye to a farther horizon—either of one's own garden, or, perhaps above eye level, of the garden next door.

In a small garden a wall or fence can create a slimmer background than trees or shrubs. Or walls

can be constructed and foliage employed to achieve a Hanging Gardens of Babylon effect. On a smaller scale, walls can be built in tiers and pots hung from them so that some plants cascade down the whole length, while others climb up—a luxuriant scene that may be just as refreshing in New York or London as it was in Babylon thousands of years ago.

In addition to a backdrop, a garden needs a focus. Perhaps it is an unusual specimen tree, such as a fragrant snowbell, *Styrax obassia*, or a rustic

bench tucked into a nook. Selecting a focus is a personal decision and often involves animals or people. For some gardens it is a well-placed birdbath or feeder. For others, it could be an intimate outdoor dining area, with a table and chairs surrounded by and decorated with plants. Other gardeners may want to banish humans from their gardens and restrain their guests on a patio, perhaps, while keeping the real garden as their private pact with nature. Here the focus might be a splendid urn full of plants, or an island border

designed to be admired but not intruded upon except by those who love it best.

A larger garden might have several focuses, with meandering paths, or orchestrated walks to carefully tended extravaganzas. These could be a prized piece of sculpture at the center of an herb or water garden, or a much loved, tender plant growing far north of its accustomed zone. Given enough room, foliage plants can function as punctuation marks in a garden. For instance, a spiky yucca or conical conifer can make sensible

A pair of characterized SARGENT'S HEMLOCKS (TSUGA CANADENSIS 'SARGENTII') soar at Meadowbrook Farm near Philadelphia.

Fine and bold textures are interwoven in a Denver garden with *Astilbe chinensis* 'Pumila', Japanese painted fern (*Athyrium goeringianum* 'Pictum') and *Hosta sieboldiana* 'Frances Williams'.

beginnings and endings to a border. In a really large bed, a collection of green vertical lines can create commas, which become welcome breathing spaces for the flustered eye. A piece of evergreen topiary, or plants such as the giant-leafed *Onopordum acanthium,* are definitely exclamation points, while trees such as the spring and autumn show-stopper Okame cherry, *Prunus* 'Okame', are worth considering to bring everyone to a complete halt.

One of the most practical uses of foliage is to disguise one's inevitable possessions, such as the trash, the motorcycle parked against the wall, or the children's plastic wading pool. Dense stands of rhododendrons, hydrangeas and hollies will hide most things. If a truly impenetrable visual barrier is needed, golden conifers like *Thuja orientalis* 'Elegantissima' are a possibility. If one has nothing more to hide than gangly lily legs or the fading foliage of spring bulbs, small mounds of grey *Santolina chamaecyparissus* or bottle green candytuft, *Iberis sempervirens,* will suffice.

Foliage can also be used to provide cohesion in a garden. It can create harmony in a small space where the color scheme may be out of sync, or act as peacemaker where the flowers are all shouting at each other. In addition, foliage is used to create both unity and repetition. For instance, the color of cream roses and yellow-flowering Stella d'Oro daylilies can be echoed by a yellow variegated shrub—hues that will reverberate gently all summer long. An echo of the bronzed purple foliage of *Berberis thunbergii* 'Atropurpurea' can be cast back and forth between the autumn seed heads of sedum 'Autumn Joy'.

Finally, foliage plants serve as supports for yet more plants. A trellis or archway is not always appropriate, and climbing plants may be just as happy crawling up a tree or through a bush.

A Plan
for All
Seasons

In a Pennsylvania garden,
the path to an urn of aloe is
flanked by LAMB'S EARS
(*STACHYS BYZANTINA*) and
maroon *SALVIA VANHOUTTII*.

Primary colors blaze with the leaves of WHITE BIRCH (*BETULA PENDULA*) and BURNING BUSH (*EUONYMUS ALATA*).

Each spring I cannot resist peeling back some scaly bud covers of emerging tree leaves, just to make sure the tiny leaves are there, and it is not some great hoax. Some winters are so long that one begins to wonder. Watching the buds of deciduous trees and shrubs grow fatter each day and finally burst open has to be one of the great joys in life. Some of the leaves briefly hang limp and appear pale, almost nervous. Then they start unfolding their pleats. I never cease to be amazed how a leaf so large can fit into a bud so small. The effect is like opening a Japanese paper sculpture—and a great relief that the leaves do not have to be stuffed back in.

Plants react to lengthening daylight hours and rising ground and air temperatures by making spurts of growth in spring. Some trees begin the reproduction process almost immediately, flowering as quickly as possible, even before the new foliage is out. Desert plants take advantage of spring rains by flowering and seeding early. Spring bulbs flower before many trees have leafed out and stolen much of the light. The earliest flowering herbaceous plants are short, because they have not had the time to grow and do not have to compete for light and air space with the profusion of taller plants that takes over later in the year. In early spring the most insignificant foliage and flowers attract the gardener's and bees' attention. The flowering of *Veronica pectinata*, woolly veronica, is a major Easter event in my garden, while in the summer, its minute blue blooms and dusky green foliage scarcely merit a second glance.

As spring progresses, foliage changes color constantly. Tremulous, delicate greens become bolder, new pale turquoise leaves turn a harder blue and pubescent, mint green leaves grow grey and hairy. For the gardener it is a time of intense excitement—a time to welcome old friends back from the soil again and wait anxiously for loved ones to reappear, lest they expired over the winter. Spring is often so hectic with planning, planting, seeding and relocating that it is sometimes a good idea just to stop and watch.

With so many diverse climates and tastes, different people aim to have their gardens peak in different months. Most gardeners, however, plan to have their garden look its best at some point in the summer. During the long, light summer days, the plants are working to reproduce and, except for annuals, to grow the maximum amount of foliage to store the maximum amount of food. Whether striving to photosynthesize under a moist, verdant green canopy, fighting for room in an herbaceous border or endeavoring to conserve moisture under hot sun, the foliage in a summer garden is constantly exerting itself to ensure success in a limited amount of time. One should help wherever possible to make sure that each plant has enough moisture, space and light and that the right chemicals are in the soil.

Having a garden is like having a class full of children. One has to discipline the boisterous and bossy plants, encourage the timid and less effective plants, attend to the most demanding ones and not neglect the ones who sit quietly at the back, all the while being thankful for those who survive and flourish in spite of one's errors.

When autumn finally arrives, a lot of chemical changes take place. As the production of green chlorophyll fades, the colors of other chemicals, such as *xanthophyll* (yellow) and *carotene* (orange), which were always present, become noticeable. *Anthocyanins* are responsible for the more red and purplish pigmentation in some foliage. Leaves turn ruddy in autumn when there are sunny days and

cold nights. Touring the New England area of the United States in October, taking in its stunning autumn foliage colors, and eating maple candy and syrup is a feast for both the eye and the stomach. Numerous trees offer gardeners a bit of New England color. After the thrills and blaze of summer color, some people find autumn a letdown. Colorful foliage such as scarlet tree leaves, however, can liven up the slowly shortening days.

Some fine examples include pin oak, *Quercus palustris,* and tupelo, also called sour gum, and black gum, *Nyssa sylvatica.* A maple with outstanding color in midwestern states such as Michigan and Illinois is *Acer rubrum,* while staghorn sumac, *Rhus typhina,* is one of several sumacs that tolerate extreme cold and dry conditions, and has magnificent sunset colors in autumn. Farther south, sourwood, also called sorrel tree, *Oxydendrum arboreum,* has white summer blooms before it turns crimson. Persian parrotia, *Parrotia persica,* and Japanese stewartia, *Stewartia pseudocamellia,* are splendid specimen trees with excellent autumn color. *Stewartia monodelpha* is a larger tree with similar beautiful white flowers, attractive winter bark and autumn coloring. Virginia creeper, *Parthenocissus quinquefolia,* while not a tree, looks great growing up one, and, with its vermilion leaves, will cheer any gardener who has the autumn blues.

In autumn the leaves of deciduous trees and shrubs are sealed off from the branches by cells at the base of the petiole, so that when the leaf drops the plant does not "bleed" to death. Only a small scar remains, often shaped like a crescent moon, that can be observed on many twigs and branches. These small spots within the abcission scar show where the veins were connected to the petiole and leaf. Once the sealing has taken place, the leaf

dies, and the gardener can do nothing but enjoy the resulting mulch that will provide cover and nutrients in the following years.

By the end of autumn plants are already prepared for next spring. It is important that plants go into winter in good health.

While autumn is a time of slowing down and dying in the garden, winter is when things appear to stop altogether. But, as with hibernation, minimal functions continue to ensure survival. In many areas where the ground is frozen, roots cannot take up moisture, and the plant relies on energy stored during previous seasons.

Winter is when the evergreens are most appreciated. Gardeners who live in cold climates rely heavily on evergreens to sustain the soul when so many signs of life are gone. Broad-leafed evergreens in particular are a solace. Manzanita, also called bearberry, *Arctostaphylos* spp., is a good example. *Mahonia japonica* with glossy, pinnate foliage, actually bears yellow flowers in winter. Later the glistening leaves and profuse blue berries remind one of the ocean, forced between rocks at high tide, spewing sprays of green and droplets of water. Many not-so-broad-leafed perennials winter over, and gardeners cherish them for their stoicism.

In winter the great conifers are a lifesaver for wildlife and trusted colleagues in the garden. When the wind whistles in the pines and the winter sun glazes the icy spruce and juniper, one remembers why one planted them. When the cold bites, people's noses turn red, and so do the leathery leaves of *Bergenia cordifolia.* Christmas is clearly the time to enjoy the reds and greens available in the garden. When the prescribed hollies, ivies and Christmas trees are flourishing, it is already time to think of snowdrops, *Galanthus* spp., hellebores, aconites and spring rituals again.

CHOKECHERRY *(PRUNUS VIRGINIANA)* leaves fall over a pair of stoical lions and *PYRACANTHA COCCINEA.*

Green Murals
and Seasonal Studies

SELECTIONS FOR BACKDROPS AND SCREENS

Berberis thunbergii (Japanese barberry) Red, green or golden-leaved varieties tolerate a wide range of conditions.

Sorbaria sorbifolia (sorbus) Deep green, pinnate leaves on dense, suckering shrubs with white fluffy summer flowers.

Taxus baccata (common yew) A classic choice for a formal garden.

Cornus alba 'Elegantissima Variegata' (dogwood) Light colored alternative to dark, evergreen backdrops.

Cotinus coggygria (smokebush) Purple or marine green leaves and smoke "puffs" for an informal planting.

SEASONAL COLOR SELECTIONS

Bergenia cordifolia (pigsqueak) Bold leaves tinted maroon and red in autumn and winter.

Geranium macrorrhizum, G. X cantabrigiense (cranesbills) Valuable late season color for weary borders and with fall-blooming crocus and colchicums.

Epimedium X *versicolor* 'Neo-sulphureum' Heart-shaped leaves feature reddish tinted leaves when yellow flowers bloom in spring.

Nandina domestica 'Firepower' (heavenly bamboo) Dwarf, green-leaved shrub features red new spring growth and fiery fall color for intimate areas.

Parthenocissus tricuspidata (Boston ivy) Spectacular autumn leaf color to cover large expanses of wall.

The silver-patterned leaves of LAMIUM MACULATUM mingle with the threadleaf foliage and pale flowers of COREOPSIS VERTICILLATA 'MOONBEAM'.

Chapter Four

The Tended Thicket

Here hills and vales, the woodland and the plain,

Here earth and water seem to strive again,

Not chaos—like together crushed and bruised,

But, as the world, harmoniously confused:

Where order in variety we see,

And where, though all things differ, all agree.

Alexander Pope, 1688–1744

ARBORS, VINES AND SHADY BOWERS

On the left overleaf, cones of variegated ivy and a cushion of *JUNIPERUS SQUAMATA* 'BLUE STAR' punctuate a boxwood-lined walk at Meadowbrook Farm. On the right overleaf, a shaded stream suits *LIGULARIA STENOCEPHALA* 'THE ROCKET', and *RODGERSIA PINNATA*.

The origins of arbors were probably practical. Around the twelfth century, monks began building cloisters to connect the parts of their abbeys and provide space for walking and for contemplation. Functional covered walkways also connected kitchens—often separated from houses to protect against fire—to the house so food could be transported even in inclement weather. In the new world, at Thomas Jefferson's Monticello in Virginia, an underground passage, lined with storage rooms and a wine cellar, connected the smokehouse and kitchen to the main house. Jefferson's thoughtfulness in protecting his slaves from the elements was considered generous at the time.

Naturally, the covered walkway, or arbor, found its way into the garden, and soon became a matter of status. Having an attractive, sheltered place to walk or sit in the garden was evidence that one had sufficient leisure time to enjoy the outdoors, to read, to entertain family and guests. An arbor sent a message that the homeowner was a civilized being, one who appreciated a quiet retreat from the sweaty threshing taking place in the fields beyond, or the noise of the marketplace. Over time there have been fashions in arbors, but their appeal has remained constant.

In sixteenth-century England, when sanitation was primitive, bowers of sweet-smelling plants were particularly useful. Around 1577 Thomas Hill wrote, "Herbars . . . not only defendeth the heat of the Sun, but yieldeth a delectable smel, much refreshing the sitters under it." Hill, a fine gardener, recommended planting arbors of six-foot-high rosemary, "wondrous sweet," jasmine, musk and damask roses, and myrtle. He spoke of "allies and walkways" with windows through which

Opposite, echoes of ivy resound in the rose garden at Ladew Topiary Gardens in Maryland.
Above, DUTCHMAN'S PIPE *(ARISTOLOCHIA DURIOR)* cloaks a pergola at Wave Hill.

people could admire the garden flowers beyond.

Much later, Queen Victoria and Prince Albert, who grew up in the forests of Germany, led a vogue for rustic gardens with arbors of logs with the bark and small branches intact. William Wordsworth, an English poet who adored the countryside, felt so deprived in winter that he planned a "green, unfading bower" of evergreen foliage in his garden.

For some landowners an arbor has served as a formal extension of a grand house, with stone columns, marble balustrades, and a roof of beams—all softened with vines such as wisteria. Other homes have favored a pergola, a foliage-covered walk from the front door to the gate, to extend a refuge to their visitors.

Sometimes an arbor is completely separate from the house and a feature of the garden—perhaps a little trellised temple in a glade. Victorian tea houses were popular in the days when ladies did not want to acquire freckles or a tan, and their long, heavy dresses kept them sitting in the shade. These were often built of wooden trellises, covered with vines and roses and located with a choice view of the garden. The most enchanting garden houses were built on a central axle and could be pivoted in any direction to take advantage of winter sunshine and some shade in July.

In cottage gardens, where there is less space, trellises and arbors have been built over wells and garden gates, and as screens between the vegetable and flower gardens. Even in the most humble railway towns of the American West, the tiny gardens of Victorian homes sported grape arbors.

Arbors remain a valid feature of the contemporary garden. City rooftop gardens and gardens in urban canyons, surrounded by tall buildings, are good candidates for covered arbors. A natural retreat can be constructed where foliage plants can flourish in filtered light, securing them a delectable haven, privacy and a supply of oxygen. Inside, shade-loving plants such as begonias and fuchsia will grow. Outside, consider *Hydrangea petiolaris,* a climbing hydrangea that copes well with pollution and has large, white inflorescences.

Out of the city a pergola trained with golden-chain tree, *Laburnum* X *watereri* 'Vossii', is a luxurious addition to any garden. The profuse racemes of yellow flowers pouring over trellis work is a spectacular sight in summer. Most arbor vines are renowned for their flowers rather than their foliage, but this combination of leaves and blossoms is irresistible.

Some of the hardiest perennial climbers are *Campsis bignonia* 'Madame Galen', a trumpet vine that produces large, waxy orange-red blossoms, and is much loved by hummingbirds. *Campsis radicans* 'Flava' has lots of primrose yellow trumpets. Grapes will cover an arbor with a thick canopy of palmately lobed leaves and pale green tendrils that reach out and tickle passersby. This handsome foliage makes perfect doilies for serving summer

Pots of IVY GERANIUM *(PELARGONIUM PELTATUM)* decorate one-of-a-kind rustic arbors at Lost Marbles Ranch.

meals, and of course dangling bunches of grapes have been sought after since the dawn of man.

The many large, brilliantly flowering clematis are a popular choice for climbing an arch or pergola. Most need to grow in full sun with their roots in the shade. 'Duchess of Edinburgh' has magnificent double white flowers in early summer. 'Ville de Lyon' bears velvety, crimson stars from midsummer onward, and a pretty little late bloomer is the sweet autumn clematis, whose creamy flowers are small but smell lovely, and whose vines are very hardy. In milder climates there is a greater choice of vines, and two worth considering are Dutchman's-pipe, *Aristolochia durior*, with great simple, heart-shaped leaves that provide more shade than most vines and sophisticated brown and white blooms, and five-leaf akebia vine, *Akebia quinata*, with smaller airy, palmately compound leaves and purple flowers.

For an informal or cottage garden, the sweet-smelling, rambling honeysuckles, *Lonicera* spp., and rambunctious silver lace vines, *Polygonum* spp., are always a success; their billowing blooms and foliage will capture the hearts of even the most unromantic. Three fast-growing annual vines that are ideal for the renter who wants an instant arbor are: cup-and-saucer vine, *Cobaea scandens;* cypress vine, *Ipomoea quamoclit,* with delicate cypress-type foliage, and separate red and white flowers on the same plant; and the old-fashioned favorite, morning-glory vine, *Ipomoea purpurea,* whose blue trumpets still thrill me when they clamber through my grapes.

Rambunctious WISTERIA FLORIBUNDA, opposite, is fronted by cosmos, APPLEBLOSSOM GRASS (*GAURA LINDHEIMERI*) and foxglove-like CERATOTHECA TRILOBA. The leaves of WINE GRAPES (*VITIS VINIFERA*), above, add texture and mass to any garden structure.

HEDGES, TOPIARY AND ESPALIERED TREES

In an organized society there is a need to define property. For at least two thousand years hedges have offered an appealing alternative to walls or fences. The Greeks and Romans used thorny hedges "to defend the injuries both of the thief and beast." During medieval times mixed hedges were sometimes trimmed to make the lower part consist of closely spaced bare branches, while the top was allowed to leaf out "to prevent poultry flying over it," according to *The Gardener's Labyrinth*, written by Thomas Hill in 1577. This was probably not beautiful but certainly practical in a limited space.

In Elizabethan England, clipped evergreen hedges enclosed orderly flower beds. They became a major design element in rigidly rectangular but charming formal gardens. Their plans were made with mathematical precision; for instance, flower beds were made the same width as the height of the wall behind them. Dark green hedges lined gravelled paths and small enclosures—filled with colored gravel or a single species of flower—as it was not acceptable to mix plants in a bed. Over time hedge patterns became increasingly elaborate.

Box, sometimes privet, and later, yew trees formed lines, scrolls and even initials. These were designed to be admired from the second-story reception rooms of the house, while the gravel paths through them prevented the proud owners from soiling the hems of their expensive and hard-to-clean clothes.

Deciduous trees, such as whitethorn and hornbeam, also appeared in hedges. Limes and hornbeams created green walkways and tunnels when their branches were woven up and over together to form an *allée verte,* an attractive and sensible precaution in a country where it often rains.

The gardens of large plantations and estates in America, and of country houses in England, were, and in some cases still are, divided into separate areas for formal entertaining and more intimate pleasures—a natural extension of the grand houses they surrounded. These open-air rooms, sheltered by tall hedges that defined the space, provided some relief from the elements and ensured privacy. Sometimes their entrances were concealed by cunningly planted foliage and shrubbery. Inside were privileged retreats—lawns for sports such as tennis and croquet, and water gardens, rose

A hedge of PRIVET *(LIGUSTRUM VULGARE)* encircles an ivy-clad sundial and *CHRYSANTHEMUM* X *MORIFOLIUM.*

Scallops of BOXWOOD
(*BUXUS SEMPERVIRENS*)
enclose LILY-OF-THE-NILE
(*AGAPANTHUS PRAECOX*
subspecies *ORIENTALIS*) in
San Francisco.

At the Pennsylvania
Horticultural Society, a
clipped row of AMERICAN
HOLLY (*ILEX OPACA*) sets the
backdrop for parterres of
DWARF JAPANESE BARBERRY
(*BERBERIS THUNBERGII*
'ATROPURPUREA NANA')
filled with COLEUS (*COLEUS*
X *HYBRIDUS*) and *COREOPSIS*
VERTICILLATA 'ZAGREB'.

gardens and sunken gardens for relaxation. Farther afield were similar enclosures for the essential kitchen gardens, orchard and greenhouses.

Connecting these gardens were paths, usually edged with flower borders and more hedges. One can imagine the warmth and sense of peace and security such a hedged environment provided. On a hot day the smell of lavender and box would be heady and delicious. Even on chilly October days, when the northern sun was weak, and the bees had abandoned the open areas, they would buzz around the leftover flowers hugged by the ancient hedges.

The view from the English country house was sometimes contrived to hide the line where one estate ended and the next began. The ideal was an uninterrupted vista from the windows, across flower borders, lawn and finally to pastures with livestock beyond. Hedges or fences would have spoiled the grand sense of space, so between the lawn and field a sharp drop of about five feet was excavated to keep the animals out of the garden. This barrier is termed a HaHa—but I have never understood if this chortling is because the cows could not jump up, or the guests could fall down.

Formal hedges became forms of amusement and decoration. Mazes were popular; Hampton Court still contains the most famous, first built in 1690 near London. Planted with hornbeam and then changed to yew, this puzzle maze has half a mile of paths. Having a garden large enough to grow hedges that are merely for getting lost in seems a delightful absurdity today.

Box and yew trees are slow growing and long lived. Some yew trees in English churchyards are reputed to be a thousand years old, and planting one now certainly shows faith in the future. There are two main sorts, the English or common yew, *Taxus baccata*, and the hardier Japanese yew, *Taxus*

cuspidata, and a hybrid between them—*Taxus* X *media*. There are many cultivars, including variegated and golden yews of all shapes and sizes.

Box can also be divided roughly into two groups: common boxwood, *Buxus sempervirens*, which originated in the Mediterranean area and suffers at temperatures below −20° F (−29° C), and littleleaf boxwood, *Buxus microphylla*, a Far Eastern native, with Korean box the most hardy.

One of the few problems with a formal hedge is the amount of space it occupies. It is usual to allow the same amount for the width as the height. One magnificent old hedge at President James Monroe's house, Ashlawn, outside Charlottesville, Virginia, is so venerable it almost overwhelms the path to the front door, but after two hundred years a little obesity can be tolerated. A clever trick for a small, modern garden is trimming a formal hedge progressively smaller to create a false perspective and an illusion of space and length.

There are two further refinements in plant obedience training: topiary and espaliered trees. Both require endless amounts of time, patience and skill. Pruning, clipping and training trees into unnatural shapes has created conflict among gardeners since Pliny the Younger mentioned topiary in the first century A.D. The debate centers on priorities in the garden—whether art or nature should have the upper hand. Opinion and fashion have swung back and forth. Should nature be allowed to proceed in all its glory, encouraged but unhampered by man, who cannot possibly improve on divine inspiration? (How noble.) Or should nature be subjugated, lest the garden flourish uncontrolled and men bare their primitive instincts and revert to wild beasts? (How thrilling.) A provocative dilemma.

Topiary are usually evergreen trees, so the hard-

won effect lasts year-round. Their sculptural quality admirably suits both period houses and contemporary, minimalist gardens. Crisp cones, obelisks and pyramids are stylish shapes that do not overly emasculate the tree. Topiary is an area, however, in which a sense of humor and personal taste can run rampant. Trees have been tortuously shorn into dragons, chessmen, peacocks, corkscrews, chairs and horses, to mention a few of the more prosaic forms.

Topiary is a valid way of creating good architectural forms with foliage in the garden year-round. It is an extension of using a fine specimen tree, with maximum control over the outcome. Some trees that lend themselves to topiary are the same boxwoods and yews that work in formal hedges, and trees such as cypress, *Cupressus sempervirens,* that grow somewhat faster. A dense hardy privet, Ligustrum grows quickly, although it is deciduous. It can be shaped easily or grown as a small standard tree. Both upright *Juniperus excelsa* 'Stricta', with spiny grey foliage, and burk red cedar, *Juniperus virginiana* 'Burkii', with soft, blue-green foliage turning purplish in winter, are tall evergreens that lend themselves to topiary work. The California incense cedar, *Calocedrus decurrens,* is for the gardener who likes to plan ahead. This tall, narrow tree tolerates clipping, grows slowly and may live from five hundred to a thousand years.

Europeans have long cultivated grape vines for the production of wine. Espaliered trees are trained like vines and pruned into artificial shapes against a wall, fence or flat frame. Years ago in England when most people with land grew their own fruit, they found that tender crops such as peaches, pears and apricots were unreliable unless planted against a south-facing protected wall. Selecting the correct branches, pruning them vigorously to produce the finest flowers and fruit and training them along wires became an art form. Dozens of designs for espaliered trees were circulated in botanical periodicals and books. Thompson's *Gardener's Assistant,* published in 1859, devoted ten pages to designs for branching fruit trees, from flat fans to three-dimensional balloons and chandelier shapes. Some of the prettiest trees were espaliered up walls into wineglass shapes, with the trunk forming the stem and the branches billowing out to form the goblet. At the coronation of Queen Elizabeth II, standard rose bushes were trained into royal crowns, complete with flowering jewels.

Espalier used to be such an important part of garden design and fruit production that gardeners could make a career in it. It remains a practical method of growing short trees and shrubs. Espaliered trees take up little space—a great advantage in a small garden. In a gentle maritime climate, they are a pleasing way to soften a hard wall with flowers, fruit and foliage. In continental climates, trees should not be grown on a southern wall; the temperatures will vary too much.

Formal gardens require level ground and flat terraces, because straight lines and patterns are an integral part of their design. Uneven ground, slopes and hills favoring winding paths, curved borders and informal hedges are ideal for many twentieth-century gardens. It is now as important to shield the yard from car headlights and noise as it was to screen a private trysting place from prying servants. Consequently, dense evergreen hedges formed from such conifers as spruce, juniper and hemlock, and broad-leafed evergreens such as Japanese holly, boxwood and cherry laurel are perennially popular. Different trees and shrubs grouped together can make an adequate screen that is not so obvious a barrier as a line of identical trees. Almost any large plant with fine foliage can be used this way, and selecting a range of heights, shapes and textures will enhance the effect. Prickly shrub roses and the hawthorn *Crataegus monogyna* have two advantages: they have lovely flowers and haws, and they deter neighboring children. Stands of bamboo are also a good way to blot out an unwanted landscape. Both dwarf forsythia, *Forsythia viridissima* 'Bronxensis', and 'Somerset' daphne, *Daphne* X *burkwoodii,* make beautiful, informal, spring-flowering hedges. Some truly exquisite hedges are found in Mobile, Alabama, where azaleas and rhododendrons line the driveways of many languid antebellum homes.

Fanciful yew sculptures at Ladew Topiary Gardens are complemented by the changing leaves of FLOWERING DOGWOOD *(CORNUS FLORIDA).*

SHADE GARDENS, WOODLANDS AND FERNS

Serenity reigns in a garden where primroses, impatiens, ajuga and hosta thrive in a shady nook.

In summer the word *shade* conjures up cool relief from the sun's rays. Whether tall trees the gardener inherited or planted create the shade, or the neighbors' house shares its shadow, the shade garden can be every bit as lovely as the sunny one. Its foliage tends to be more luxuriant, and a shady nook or sheltered glade can be a welcome refuge. Even a single shaded bed can be turned to great advantage. The shade garden offers an opportunity to grow different plants in a microclimate distinct from a sunny bed just a few yards away.

Many beautiful plants welcome shade; they have adapted to reduced sunlight and reach their full flowering and reproducing potential without direct sun. Other plants will grow in shade, but unhappily. Their physical and chemical composition prevents them from functioning properly when out of the sun's rays; they grow leggy and may not flower. Many shade-tolerant plants have larger leaves than their sun-loving colleagues, because they need to present a greater area to the light for photosynthesis to take place. These same plants in bright sunlight will scorch and wilt. Some plants will grow in deep shade, while others require dappled shade or a portion of sun each day. Certain plants demand cool, moist shade, while different groups can cope with a dry, shaded area or warm, wet conditions. Analyzing these variables is part of what makes gardening so interesting.

The leaves and branches of overhead deciduous trees produce the most enchanting shade. In winter bare branches make minimal shadows, allowing the low winter sun to shine through, while summer sunlight falls between leaves in checkered patches. This environment is perfect for a wide range of plants.

The more hectic one's life-style, the more a woodland glade may appeal to the senses. It can be anything from a small wild portion of the garden to a sober section of a carefully laid out, shaded formal garden. It might be a small island in a lawn, with specimen trees and shrubs and with shade-loving plants on the north side of the bed. A little woodland on the southern border of a small property, perhaps against a wall or fence, will allow the deciduous trees to shade the house in summer and provide cool north-facing shade at their feet. If there is enough room for a deep woodland, one can incorporate an underplanting of shade-tolerant shrubs, perennials and ground covers along meandering paths.

In the selection of woodland plants, the type of soil is as important as the type of shade. In traditional native woodland and forest, there may be thousands of years of accumulation of leaf mold and an acidic soil. If the shade garden is carved out of an ancient wood, the soil may not be a problem. Difficulties may arise, however, if acid-loving plants such as rhododendron and trillium are planned for a woodland glade in an area that historically has had few trees.

Other considerations in a woodland are the density of the canopy, the tree root system and the colors of the foliage. When strong, dark shade is desired, large-leafed trees, shrubs and dense evergreens are appropriate. If one wants underplantings of shrubs, flowering perennials and spring bulbs, then smaller-leafed, airier tall trees should be planted to permit sufficient sunlight to penetrate below. Trees such as birches, *Betula*, provide light shade. Pin oak, *Quercus palustris*, *Robinia pseudoacacia* and fern leaf beech, *Fagus sylvatica* 'Asplenifolia', will allow dappled shade, as will a small buckeye such as *Aesculus parviflora*, an airy English holly tree like *Ilex aquifolium*

'Pyramidalis', and, in a less traditional setting, *Ginkgo biloba* or one of the many eucalypti. Orchard trees form lovely woodland scenes, and any of the breathtaking, spring-blooming fruit trees such as *Prunus sargentii* or *Malus* 'Professor Sprenger' create only light shade.

The problem with shallow-rooted trees such as beeches is that they absorb so much moisture from the top layers of the soil that the smaller-foliage plants have difficulty thriving under them. Oaks, however, have a deeper root system that makes them difficult to transplant but forgiving about underplantings. Finally, one has a choice of colored foliage to consider. The light to mid-greens tend to look best in garden woodlands, as they allow the sun to shine through the translucent leaves. The top layer of the garden should be pale and light, growing emerald in midlayers, with the fiercest, blackest greens saved for ground covers.

In a classical woodland setting with acidic soil, a broad range of foliage material will grow under the taller trees. Rhododendrons, with their handsome sprays of green foliage and magnificent spring blooms, deserve their immense popularity. There are hundreds of species and cultivars. Only a few species of mountain laurel, *Kalmia latifolia*, exist, but all have glossy evergreen foliage and small waxy flowers that make them a joy for flower arranging in spring. Vibernums, pieris and witch hazel, *Hamamelis*, will also flourish in these woods. Finding a wild azalea is always exciting; planting an azalea garden is an ideal. With the many plants available today, gardeners can create an even more magnificent formal or wild woodland.

Spring bulbs and early flowering perennials are a natural in a wooded area. They emerge from a thick blanket of dead brown leaves to form a green carpet of foliage and flowers that blooms in the fresh spring light filtering through the bare branches above. Bulbs can be planted in drifts to evoke a natural woodland or in more structured beds in a formal woodland garden. Hellebores may have wintered over in milder climates; most have handsome, palmately divided foliage and greenish white or dusky maroon flowers that look equally at home beside an elegant townhouse or in a wild wood. Some of the many species of snowdrop, *Galanthus,* will also bloom in spring, quickly followed by crocus, chionodoxa, daffodils, little checkered lilies *(Fritillaria)* and *Erythronium.* To my mind, a woodsy bed is not a real wood unless it has lots of primroses pushing up minute points of lime green that soon unfurl into crinkly rosettes. One of the prettiest is a hardy primula from the Himalayas, *Primula denticulata,* sporting long stems and a mop of mauve flowers whose petals look as if they have been cut with pinking shears. More plants to weave into this spring tapestry are the heart-shaped leaves of sweet violets, *Viola odorata,* wild ginger, *Asarum europaeum,* with glossy, round leaves; woodland phlox, *Phlox stolonifera,* and lily-of-the-valley.

As spring progresses, the pastel colors of flowers gleam against the dusky shadows of foliage and the dark trunks of trees. The large rosettes of foxglove foliage are among the first to send up tall racemes of waxy blooms, rising above the American native foamflower, *Tiarella cordifolia,* and *Anemone blanda* from southeast Europe. Among the plants grown particularly for their fine foliage, although they do flower, are the pulmonarias, some of which have spotted leaves; *Pachyphragma macrophylla,* which has large, round leaves and offers a good contrast to much of the other spring foliage; and *Euphorbia robbiae,* one of the few euphorbias that will grow in shade. The foliage of

Arum italicum 'Pictum' stands out beautifully in the growing sea of green. Its glossy, sagittate leaves look like green marble with creamy, reticulate venation in early spring, but they die back during the summer.

The blue-green deeply scalloped foliage of columbine would be worth cultivating even if the flowers were not so heavenly. In June in the Rocky Mountains, carpets of *Aquilegia caerulea* present their blue and white flowers under the aspens and conifers. In the sixteenth century, the renowned artist Albrecht Dürer immortalized the columbine in an exquisite botanical illustration of *Aquilegia vulgaris,* and they have been popular ever since. The yellow and red flowers of *Aquilegia canadensis* and *A. formosa* echo the foliage of variegated hybrid hostas such as 'Yellow Splash'.

The shady woodland garden becomes a refuge during a hot summer. The water expired by millions of leaves functions as a swamp cooler, lowering the temperature while increasing the humidity. The top tier of leaves becomes thicker, increasing the shade, and there are fewer flowers in the lower layers. The tall spires of bugbane, *Cimicifuga racemosa,* and others, glow delightfully in the green gloom. Great golden candles of *Ligularia stenocephala* 'The Rocket' look especially dramatic against evergreen trees. Aruncus and astilbe wave their soft plumes in a gentle summer breeze while they wait for fireflies to flit among their lacy foliage.

During a heat wave, just looking at enormous green foliage can make one feel cooler. While the sunny garden simmers, the woodland is at its most verdant, with a lavish display of abundant leaves. Two plants with leaves big and round enough to be umbrellas are mayapple, *Podophyllum peltatum,* and *Astilboides tabularis,* formerly known as *Rodgersia tabularis.* On a sizzling hot day no plant appears

In a cliff garden, pines tower over ferns and native plants of Montana.

Y ELLOW ARCHANGEL
(*LAMIASTRUM
GALEOBDOLON*), ferns and
variegated *PIERIS JAPONICA*
hug the foundation of a
Vancouver home.

more frigid than the shade-loving hostas. There are many kinds in all sizes and textures, but all grow with a crisp, calm restraint that seems to pour cold water on even the most torrid afernoon.

Among the many ground covers that grow well in the shade, big blue lilyturf, *Liriope muscari,* is a good choice for a formal garden. The cultivar 'Silver Sunproof' has dapper yellow and green-striped leaves, and these neat bunches of grass-like foliage appear equally sharp in individual clumps or as an edging to a shaded border. Creeping Forget-Me-Not, *Omphalodes verna,* is more casual with bright blue flowers and a mass of simple green leaves.

Ferns are primitive plants that do not flower, but reproduce asexually by means of spores. These can sometimes be observed as a fine, brown powder emitted from the back of some of the leaves, but

gardeners find it easier to increase ferns by division. Nearly all ferns need to grow in part shade, preferably with rich humus and consistently moist soil. Fern leaves are called fronds, and new leaves are sometimes called fiddleheads, as they emerge rolled up like the carved head of a violin.

Ferns have been grown in gardens for so long that many superstitions exist about them. In the sixteenth century Thomas Hill gave the following advice in *The Gardener's Labyrinth*: "the leaves of Fern do chase away the Serpent . . . yea and force them to change their lodgings from the Garden ground or field." Most ferns grow in a basal rosette, with large leaves divided several times into tiny, opposite leaflets. This gives them a feathery appearance, evoked by such names as shuttlecock and ostrich plume. Ferns come in all sizes, from a few inches high to noble tree ferns like the *Dicksonia antarctica,* which can be grown in woodlands in mild climates.

The delicate patterns and textures of woodland ferns contrast well with broader-leafed plants like hostas and are the perfect foil for the waxy blooms and foliage of spring bulbs and woodland lilies. Ferns' graceful habits make them desirable plants, and some gardeners devote areas to a selection of ferns that cascade over rocks, lie languidly under shrubs, and grow in trees.

A few ferns have smooth green leaves without divisions, such as the hart's-tongue fern, *Phyllitis scolopendrium,* a native to Britain. It has long, glossy fronds that make one wonder what a deer's tongue really looks like. The maidenhair fern, *Adiantum pedatum,* has a timeless appeal but a Victorian image, like lily-of-the-valley. Its delicate texture is wondrously different from any other plant. Another distinctive plant is the Japanese painted fern, *Athyrium goeringianum* 'Pictum', whose leaves are green, silvery grey and a burgundy color. In a wild woodland the purplish flowers of some digitalis and fritillaria will complement this fern, and it would have finesse in a formal shade garden paired with the wine-colored blossoms of *Helleborus orientalis* or *H. purpurascens*.

More informal, and with the great advantage of being an evergreen, is the so-called Christmas fern, *Polystichum acrostichoides*. It will grow in deep shade and sends up bright new fronds each spring. The large, lacy foliage of the ostrich, cinnamon and sensitive ferns prefers a wet, shady environment. *Osmunda cinnamomea* has fiddleheads covered with soft hairs, like a reddish brown beard. It looks lovely by a stream in a bosky dell, surrounded by bright green mosses.

The hay-scented fern, *Dennstaedtia punctilobula*, also enjoys a damp, shaded situation, but it is tough and will cope with invading tree roots and bright sun. It makes a good ground cover, and when cut down has the fragrant smell of new-mown hay. Among the hardiest ferns are the *Dryopteris* species. They include the male fern *D. filix-mas*, which tolerates dry shade in a manly way. *Polypodium vulgare* is a British native evergreen fern that will grow in the crevices of wall and rock gardens, where it spills over the stones gracefully.

Many ferns are easy to grow and adaptable, and all make good ground cover for wildlife. Some ferns have rhizomes so strong and invasive that the plants are used as a bulwark against erosion. Some ferns will tolerate lime soil, and many deciduous ferns turn a golden brown in autumn. In the old days, dried bracken ferns were collected in autumn to stuff mattresses and strew on the floor. They are also excellent container plants and

invaluable on the north side of a house, where they may thrive in spite of neglect.

The type of shade provided by buildings is different from the canopy created by trees. The soil is usually open to the sky, and plants do well without the filtered light. In addition, they may receive reflected light from neighboring structures. The north side of a house gives good shade, because the temperature is more constant than on the other sides, where excessive variations of heat and cold can be stressful to plants. Along with ferns, ivies flourish here, as well as a few bamboos, such as the arrow bamboo, *Pseudosasa japonica*. Cyclamens, such as *Cyclamen hederifolium*, interspersed with silvery dead nettles such as *Lamium maculatum* 'White Nancy', can create a charming, relatively carefree, shady bed.

This tapestry of green includes WILD GINGER (*ASARUM EUROPAEUM*), BAMBOO (*ARUNDINARIA VIRIDISTRIATIA*), IRISH MOSS (*SAGINA SUBULATA*), LADY'S MANTLE (*ALCHEMILLA MOLLIS*) and ferns.

Tending the Thicket

SELECTED CLIMBING PLANTS

Phaseolus coccineus (scarlet runner bean) Annual edible ornamental for fence or brush teepee.

Campsis radicans (trumpet vine) Impressive in bloom, but its glossy leaves are an all-season asset on sturdy structures.

Actinidia kolomikta Pink and cream leaf markings most prominent in full sun on walls or solid fence.

SELECTIONS FOR HEDGES

Ligustrum vulgare 'Lodense' (privet) Compact growth lends itself to manicured geometry.

Taxus cuspidata 'Densiformis' (dwarf yew) A good choice for a low, formal hedge, even in shade.

Lavandula angustifolia (English lavender) An unclipped, blooming row is ideal for lining walks.

Buxus sempervirens (boxwood) Versatile grower for enclosures and parterres.

SELECTED WOODLAND PLANTS

Asarum europaeum (wild ginger) Good to tuck under and around larger plants such as hostas.

Athyrium goeringianum 'Pictum' (Japanese painted fern) A short fern A with unique coloration for front of the border and nooks.

Brunnera macrophylla (heartleaf) Tough, shade-tolerant spreader with true blue flower sprays in spring.

A white-edged hosta catches glints of light with WILD GINGER *(ASARUM CANADENSE)* snuggled beneath it in a woodland planting in the Roaring Fork Valley.

Chapter Five

The Mirrored Surface

I sing of brooks, of blossoms,
birds and bowers. . . .

Robert Herrick, 1591–1674

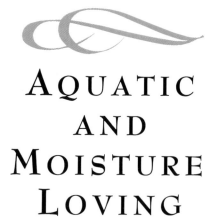

AQUATIC
AND
MOISTURE
LOVING
PLANTS

The Victorians once balanced children on the immense pads of *VICTORIA AMAZONICA*, above left, but visitors to the New York Botanical Gardens are discouraged from attempting this feat today.

Vertical CATTAILS *(TYPHA LATIFOLIA)*, below left, accent the striking leaves of ELEPHANT EARS *(COLOCASIA ESCULENTA.)*

Man has an instinctive desire to be close to water, and every garden is enhanced by a shimmering surface and the sound of trickling water. Birdbaths, ponds and waterfalls, streams and lakes are all magnets for wildlife, and they refresh the human soul. There are two kinds of water gardens: man-made pools and natural bodies of water. Either can be in sun or shade, but the man-made structure can be surrounded by any type of soil, or a path, lawn or flower border, while the natural body of water will have wet banks that host a variety of moisture-loving plants, and damp areas beyond the water's edge. A water garden might be beside a duck pond, in a low-lying area with natural bogs or beside a stream or river with sloping banks.

Large ponds and lakes can support massive plantings of huge-foliaged plants. They look magnificent with cascading waterfalls and brick or stone arched bridges, smothered in ferns and vines. Streams can be dammed into diminutive pools, and coaxed down slopes to splash onto rocks and down little falls. They need a log so one can cross them, and small plants to ooze along the seeping banks. The attraction of reflecting pools is their static, glassy surface, sometimes broken by frothing fountains and highlighted with sculpture that suggest a more formal arrangement of plants. The Japanese have perfected the art of beautifully restrained gardens using bridges and stepping stones, which represent aspects of their cultural beliefs. Regardless of a garden's size, a water garden can create a peaceful rustic enclave or an architectural masterpiece that differs completely from the environment beyond—a dramatic surprise to astonish and delight the visitor.

Plants that grow naturally beside water need a lot of moisture. They tend to have large leaves and glossy surfaces, and they are more fleshy, green and luxuriant than drought-tolerant plants. Because of their magnitude, these leaves must be sheltered from the wind or they may be torn to pieces. There is not much diversity of color, but a good deal of variation in shape.

Some garden plants grow in drier areas but grow more profusely when placed permanently in a moist situation. Other foliage prefers shade but will tolerate sun as long as its roots are consistently moist. The roots of all plants, except truly aquatic ones, will rot, however, if left in standing water. For many water-loving plants, the amount of shade and sun and the type of soil are critical to their thriving.

If a gardener has water and wants to make a wildlife habitat, or lives in the city or on a suburban lot and longs for a more natural prospect, there is a large assortment of native and cultivated plants available. Trees dripping with country charms, such as the weeping willow, *Salix babylonica*, and Young's weeping birch, *Betula pendula* 'Youngii', drape themselves gracefully over water. These trees conjure up images of Toad of Toad Hall floating by on his leaf boat, disembarking on a patch of pickerel weed, *Pontederia cordata*, and diving beneath the cattails, *Typha latifolia* (both of which will grow wild in the water). Beside a townhouse pond, a compact flowering cherry such as *Prunus serrulata* 'Shogetsu' would be appropriate.

There is much fine green foliage and a raft of pastel-colored flowers that can enliven this pastoral scene. Water dock is the giant version of its smaller cousins, with long, rumpled leaves and tall, knobby spikes of cream flowers that grow rust colored as summer progresses. This dock makes a rural statement beside water. Sensitive and

On the left overleaf, reflections of the Orient—TANYOSHO or JAPANESE UMBRELLA PINE (*PINUS DENSIFLORA* 'UMBRACULIFERA') and water lilies—characterize the Japanese garden at Denver Botanic Gardens. On the right overleaf, reflections of rustling grass at Wave Hill highlight the use of ornamental grasses.

crested wood ferns, *Onoclea sensibilis* and *Dryopteris intermedia*, will cling to wet banks and spread their long fronds across the water. Yellow flags, *Iris pseudacorus*, provide stiff vertical lines in a rolling landscape.

Informal banks of ponds and streams look lovely smothered in the bright green foliage and pink flowers of native American Joe-Pye weed, *Eupatorium purpureum*, and turtlehead, *Chelone obliqua*. Tucked into their shade, the little blue flowers of forget-me-not, *Myosotis scorpioides*, a candelabra primula like *Primula japonica*, and the chartreuse flowering *Euphorbia palustris* add color and texture to a water garden. Palustris means bog- or swamp-loving; hence many of these plants have this word as part of their scientific name.

Farther back from the bank, but still in moist soil and preferably light shade, white hellebore, *Veratrum viride*, flourishes. The unusual, oval-shaped leaves of this tall plant are a clear lime green, neatly pleated along the parallel venation. A similar height and splendid contrast would be provided by the towering branches and great palmately compound leaves of *Angelica archangelica*.

The dappled shade at the edge of a woodland garden is an ideal place for a manufactured pool or natural pond, surrounded by a choice selection of shade-loving perennials with beautiful foliage. To create the effect of a small waterfall cascading out of the woods, try a rippling, layered, blue-green hosta, interspersed with the prolific foliage and pale pink, bottle-brush flowers of *Polygonum bistorta* 'Superbum', showers of ferns and the dainty, divided leaves and blue flowers of Jacob's-ladder, *Polemonium caeruleum*. Low-growing *Brunnera macrophylla* 'Variegata' has creamy, heart-shaped leaves with broad brush strokes of green emphasizing its palmate venation. It will flourish in

a lightly shaded, moist environment, as will Turk's-cap lilies and gently fluffy-blooming astilbe, aruncus and filipendula. For exquisite detail turn over a purple-backed leaf of *Ligularia clivorum* 'Desdemona', and admire the strong rufous venation, reminiscent of the roof of a glorious Gothic cathedral with soaring stone arches glowing pink from a stained-glass window.

A water garden in bright sunlight creates a completely different feeling, with dazzling light reflecting back and forth from the sky to the water surface. The blue and gold sparkle can be echoed in the spikes of blue-flowered *Iris sibirica*, yellow grass *Carex stricta* 'Bowle's Golden', and dwarf golden bamboo *Arundinaria viridistriata*, all of which enjoy moist soil. Perhaps the most admired aquatic plant, water lilies need full sun to flower. Hardy water lilies are perennial, and except in the coldest climates can be left to winter over in the underwater tubs they were planted in. Tropical water lilies are only annuals in northern Europe and North America, but they have many advantages. They bloom in a vast array of sizes and colors, and the great waxy flowers are held aloft on strong stems, often through September. Their powerful fragrance wafts across the water with a tropical sensuality. There are just as many distinctive sizes and colors of lily pads, from small emerald saucers and variegated plum-colored plates to great bronzed platters. In fact, there is a water lily for every type of garden. They squeeze into cottage gardens and into whisky barrels of water on patios; they float in the tiniest backyard pool, and the celebrated night-blooming water lilies crumple the defenses of even the most urbane city sophisticate.

A large formal water garden can support large foliage on a grand scale. Great clumps of bamboo,

Hostas and hydrangeas accent the formality of a reflecting pool.

The old foundation of a water cistern serves as a home for iris, WATER LETTUCE (*PISTIA STRATIOTES*), PAPYRUS (*CYPERUS PAPYRUS*), and frogs—both ornamental replicas and living ones.

such as fountain grass bamboo, *Sinarundinaria nitida,* with dashing, arching dark stems and slender evergreen foliage, can form an orderly background. The royal fern, *Osmunda regalis,* is aptly named. Its majestic six-foot-high fronds will arc over fountains and actually grow in water or on a bank. Promethean stands of perennial *Gunnera chilensis*

rise up beside the water in summer. The vast, thick crinkled leaves with frilled margins are about six feet across. To achieve this great size in a few weeks, they need to absorb great quantities of water and must be grown in deep, rich loam. They are magnificent, amusing plants.

Dramatic white arum lilies, such as *Zantedeschia*

aethiopica and yellow-spathed *Lysichiton americanum* pose beside water in a manner suitable for a formal garden. The foliage of the handsome rodgersias can hold its own on any social occasion. The new red leaves of *Rheum parmatum atrosanguineum* are suitably grandiose to disguise its humble origins as a member of the rhubarb family.

Finally, water gardens are the perfect setting for jokes. In Chatsworth, England, a seventeenth century fountain built to look like a willow tree can be activated to spray a shower of water over unsuspecting guests as they pass by. A trick that might instigate a lawsuit today was considered good clean fun in Shakespeare's time.

A planting of pines, junipers and iris is carefully tended, yet designed to catch the essence of a natural streamside planting.

Reflections in the Mirrored Surface

SELECTED AQUATIC AND MOISTURE LOVING PLANTS

Pistia stratiotes (water lettuce) Floating, soft green foliage for pool or small container.

Nelumbo nucifera (sacred lotus) Platelike leaves are held aloft with pink flowers followed by unusual seed pods.

Trapa natans (water chestnut) Diamond-shaped leaves are marked with red and form-floating rosettes.

Myriophyllum aquaticum (parrot's-feather) Finely divided blue-green leaves in whorls on partially submerged stems, for small ponds.

SELECTIONS FOR WATERFALLS AND STREAMBANKS

Houttuynia cordata **'Chamaeleon'** Marginal water plant to cover moist expanses; needs some sun to enhance coloration.

Iris pseudacorus (yellow flag) The variegated form is especially pretty at water's edge, but its coloration fades in summer.

Typha latifolia (cattail) Invasive but valuable vertical element.

Pontederia cordata (pickerel weed) Glossy, dark green leaves with spikes of blue flowers late in the season.

---

*D*APHNE X *BURKWOODII* 'CAROL MACKIE' **tops the headwaters of a waterfall, also planted with bright** MEXICAN PHLOX *(PHLOX MESOLEUCA),* PINKS *(DIANTHUS spp.)* **and woolly** ROCK JASMINE *(ANDROSACE LANUGINOSA).*

Chapter Six

A Place in the Sun

He who becomes impassioned of a flower,
a blade of grass, a butterfly's wing, a nest,
a shell, wraps his passion around a small thing
that always contains a great truth.

Maurice Maeterlinck,
1862–1949

ORNAMENTAL GRASSES
AND GROUND COVERS

On the left overleaf, FOUNTAIN GRASS (*PENNISETUM SETACEUM*), rustles above BLACK-EYED SUSAN (*RUDBECKIA HIRTA*). On the right overleaf, dark-toned *PENNISETUM SETACEUM* 'RUBRUM' expands the color range of ornamental grasses.

Planting ornamental grasses is the last thing many gardeners think about, but it should be one of the first. Grass is a broad term for a host of linear-leafed plants that can form some of the most sculptural and interesting shapes. Most reeds, sedges and grasses enjoy sun and need space around them to show off the gracefulness of their leaves and their many moods. These versatile plants shine in a dry garden with sedums, cacti and agave; they gleam in a water garden and glow in woodlands; and the short ones make excellent ground covers.

The popular reasons for enjoying ornamental grasses are the practical ones. They are relatively easy perennials to look after—some need grooming only in spring. Many will adapt to different soils and light conditions. Some are drought tolerant, and they exist in virtually every size from under twelve inches (30.5 cm) to twelve feet (3.7 m).

There are, however, other more subtle reasons for liking grasses. Most flower but are pollinated by wind, so they do not need bright-colored or fragrant flowers to attract the animal kingdom to their reproductive parts. Although their blooms are inconspicuous, many grasses have spectacular seed heads, whose shapes and colors can be incorporated into the design of the garden and are much sought after for flower arrangements. Another appealing feature of grasses is their shimmering movement. Because the leaves are so narrow and the seeds minute, grasses shift in a breath of breeze, scattering light and shade.

A few grasses grow stiffly, like soldiers at attention, and make masculine, vertical accents in the garden. Others flutter and whisper in a feminine fashion. Their leaves roll and cascade down gently, making lithe loops and curves that lend sinuous lines to a flower bed. In a gentle wind, grass leaves swish and rustle, one of the garden's most soothing lullabies. When combined with the twittering of sleepy birds in the bushes and the hum of bees on their last evening rounds of the blossoms, grasses sound exquisitely soporific.

If the sounds and shapes of grasses do not captivate the gardener, the colors will. Grasses look especially handsome silhouetted against a dark background, such as coniferous evergreen trees. Particularly in winter, when the grasses' leaves and stems are dry and bleached pale blond, this beige and bottle green color combination can be striking. Glimmering shades of autumn grass color can also echo and enhance the architecture of buildings. In urban situations, where there is not much room for many plants, a single specimen of fine grass can be effective. The bold foliage of one of the many varieties of maiden grass, *Miscanthus sinensis,* can cast dramatic shadows against a wall or soften a city landscape. The horizontally striped varieties *M. s.* 'Strictus' and *M. s.* 'Zebrinus' are some of the best-looking grasses. Some clever results can be achieved by placing them near stuccoed walls and railings.

Some grasses have distinctive coloring. Bowles's golden grass, *Milium effusum* 'Aureum', is a definite yellow that grows best in light shade. The low-growing beautiful Japanese grass *Hakonechloa macra* 'Aureola' is striped green and lemon colored. Both cast golden sprays of light into a dim garden. The leaves of most grasses are translucent and lend themselves to stunning backlighting. Discreetly placed electric lights can create amazing effects beside plantings of ornamental grasses, with their beams aimed up into the foliage, spotlighting some swaying silver plumes against a dark sky. Grasses can also be grown next to a patio, where they will

be lit at night. Perhaps best of all, grasses can be planted in the open on the western edge of a garden where the setting sun will shine through their stems and foliage and glint on the seed heads. Short Japanese blood grass, *Imperata cylindrica* 'Red Baron' or 'Rubra', has rusty red foliage that glows like flames during sunset, while red straw bush, *Panicum virgatum* 'Rotschralbusch', looks like a forest fire in autumn.

For gardeners too hot under the collar to begin with, a cool chartreuse green grass with cream stripes might be the answer. Manna grass, *Glyceria maxima* 'Variegata', is happiest growing in a sunny location in a bog or beside water. Its foliage is tinged with rose early in spring and would look fresh and pretty next to pink primulas in a water garden. There are many other grasses and sedges that prefer a moist situation. A small one that flourishes in a shady wet woodland is Japanese sedge, *Carex morrowii* 'Variegata', which is green with a silver margin and combines nicely with hostas and ferns.

Blue avena, sometimes called blue oat grass, *Helictotrichon sempervirens,* is another colored grass that fits well into a border and is excellent for massing as a large blue ground cover. If *Little House on the Prairie* gives one a feeling of nostalgia, there are grasses that will transport one right back to the plains. Green Indian grass, *Sorghastrum nutans,* is as handsome as the nomadic tribes that roamed the land it covered. Northern sea oats, *Chasmanthium latifolium,* has nodding graceful seed heads that are enchanting in a prairie garden, an idyllic meadow or a flower border.

Some of the tallest grasses could be called "hotel grasses," because they are reminiscent of stately British hotels ensconced on sloping lawns. On either side of stone steps leading up to an

A bristly garden of grasses, opposite, features MISCANTHUS SINENSIS in the foreground and PENNISETUM ALOPECUROIDES.

Contrasting partners— MISCANTHUS SINENSIS 'STRICTUS' and HYDRANGEA MACROPHYLLA 'VARIEGATA' —above, repeat each other's variegation.

A carpet of bright *VERBENA TENERA* and *V. TENUISECTA* (now *GLANDULARIA TENUISECTA)* are set off by the golden sprays of LOVE GRASS *(ERAGROSTIS TRICHODES).*

imposing front door would be a great pampas grass specimen, *Cortaderia selloana,* nodding its snowy plumes to the debutantes who tripped by with ostrich feathers in their hair. Seventy-five years later the South American pampas grass is still grand when given enough room to stand in splendor. Another elegant giant is ravenna grass, *Erianthus ravennae,* which can grow to fourteen feet high with sufficient moisture. It is hardier than pampas grass, and its towering presence is magnificent beside great boulders or a waterfall. The commanding appearance and upright habit of very tall reeds like *Arundo donax* and grasses such as *Stipa gigantea* complement the contrasting forms of garden features such as a formal pool, a manicured path or pieces of topiary.

Many grasses are evergreen, or almost, and will exhibit their seed heads through much of the winter. Rising above the hibernating perennials, and rustling their desiccated foliage beside bare branches in January, they are justly admired and a great asset to any garden.

There are a number of myths about ground covers, including the following:

- Ground covers are planted only where nothing else will grow
- Gardeners only tolerate ground covers because they keep out weeds and are trouble-free
- Ground covers are boring

There is a smattering of truth to the first two myths, but number three is a fallacy. Ground covers can be as colorful and full of texture and architectural interest as any other plants in the garden.

Ground cover is a broad term encompassing thousands of plants that conceal the earth. All the usual considerations apply when selecting them, such as shade or sun tolerance, soil type, moisture and temperature range. Ground cover comes in three types: those that can be walked on, those forming a thick low carpet and taller ground covers. Because a garden always contains a series of microclimates, it is often possible to grow ground covers that would not survive in a similar climate in the wild. With a little extra protection from wind or sun, however, a bit more moisture or some amended soil, it may be possible to grow something unusual and appealing. The space available for ground covers determines their selection, too. Some look perfect covering a few square feet, while others, like the heaths and heathers, will happily veil an acre of property.

Often the most successful ground covers are mixed plantings. Mingling colored foliage of similar but not identical heights and various textures is where the real artistry and inventiveness begins. The ideal is unusual combinations and juxtapositions of plants that will make one's carpet a little bit different from all the others in the world. This is an exciting challenge, but in the scale of gardening hurdles, one of the easier ones to jump, because many ground covers flourish readily once established and require less maintenance and fewer makeovers than other parts of the garden.

Most ground covers are evergreen. Some keep their foliage most of the year, or in all but the harshest winters (the point is to make a year-round tapestry). Many plants mentioned below have variegated cultivars that enable gardeners to paint a canvas of whites and creams, along with the mixed greens and multicolored flowers.

The only ground cover that will stand up to football games and garden parties is the traditional grass lawn. There are, however, low ground covers that will cope with occasional footfalls, will rarely trip the sure-footed and do not require mowing. An excellent choice is bird's-eye veronica, *Veronica filiformis,* which forms a velvety mat of minute, round bright green leaves and is starred with speedwell blue flowers. Woolly thyme, *Thymus pseudolanuginosus,* is also nearly flat, and woolly veronica, *Veronica pectinata,* is only a bit thicker. Both have foliage that turns purplish in winter. The leaves of woolly thyme may be the smallest in the garden, and one needs spectacles to see its pinkish flowers, but it inches along flagstones or brickwork, gently enveloping other plants to form a smoky green layer that is soft to the touch. On my terrace both these plants poke pale flowers among pink-leafed sedums and hirsute, dark green-leafed and yellow-flowered shaggy hawkweed, *Hieracium villosum,* to weave a pastel carpet prettier than any rug inside the house. Pussy-toes, *Antennaria rosea,* is an alpine ground cover whose name derives from its furry flowers. Its grey suede leaves are soft enough for one's own pink feet.

The juicy, succulent leaves of some of the ice plants, *Delosperma,* will be crushed by footsteps, but they make such a striking ground cover and tolerate such hot, dry conditions that they are still worth growing. Ice plants form fast-growing mats of waxy foliage, with composite flowers that open as the sun strikes them. In spring, *D. nubigenum* has yellow flowers, while *D. cooperi* enlivens summer with fluorescent purplish-pink flowers.

The next layer of plants mentioned is too shaggy to be walked on but is still only a few inches high. While none of the plants is large and compelling enough to form vast ground covers on its own, when planted amongst each other they form a rich bejewelled surface. The miniature, turquoise-grey, pointed leaves of many dwarf pinks,

Dianthus spp., and the grass-like leaves of sea pinks, *Armeria maritima,* are a fine foil for the succulent grey leaves of *Euphorbia myrsinites.* The tiny silver leaves of partridge feather (*Tanacetum densum* var. *amani*) have a refined and dainty texture that catches the light. In contrast Mt. Atlas daisy, *Anacyclus depressus,* forms a flat rosette of dark green foliage, as lacy as a paper doily. Nestled in the middle are crimson buds that fling open to reveal starry white flowers. One could augment this group with many of the hardy stonecrops and houseleeks, which add waxy rosettes to the carpet, and then *Phlox subulata,* whose mounds looks like green hedgehogs when they are not covered with spring blooms. Lastly, for a touch

At the Strybing Arboretum, BUGLE WEED *(AJUGA REPTANS)* drowns in BABY'S TEARS *(HELXINE SOLEIROLII,* now *SOLEIROLIA SOLEIROLII).*

time without attention. In a smaller space one or two look exceedingly handsome when planted with spring bulbs. The dusky-hued rough greenery makes the waxy blooms appear even more fragile and luminous. Junipers such as *Juniperus horizontalis* 'Glauca' form wavelets of ocean blue foliage that have been likened to an expensive wool rug. One variety of hemlock, *Tsuga canadensis* 'Pendula', will flop gracefully over rocks, and a low-growing yew, *Taxus baccata* 'Repandens', is one of the rare ground covers to tolerate dry shade. Other plants that are not fussy in this difficult situation are sweet woodruff, *Asperula odorata,* some of the hardy ivies and *Euonymus fortunei* 'Sunshine', one of the creeping evergreen stalwarts.

Enjoying shade, but needing moisture, broad-leafed hostas and whorls of pachysandra make fine ground covers, especially with the contrasting foliage of ferns. One sees this combination frequently, because it works so well.

Ground covers are often used on large banks for erosion control and to provide intriguing plays of color, light and shade. Creeping mahonia, *Mahonia repens,* a very low shrub native to North America and Canada, works well in these circumstances. It has attractive foliage and sprays of small yellow flowers. *Berberis wilsoniae* is a member of the huge barberry family. It has beautiful low, arching branches, coral-colored berries and is semi-evergreen. *Berberis verruculosa* is an equally good-looking ground cover, with its glossy green leaves with white undersides. There are many heathers, but the snow heather, *Erica carnea,* is admired for its shiny foliage and long blooming period and would be a fine companion for the barberries on a bank. Lawns should be a monochromatic, soothing green, but the surrounding ground cover can be as lively as the gardener wishes.

A living mortar of orange-tinted *SEMPERVIVUM CARNEUM,* pale green *JOVIBARBA ARENARIA* and gossamer-laced *SEMPERVIVUM ARACHNOIDEUM,* known as the COBWEB HOUSELEEK, cement a planting in the rock alpine garden at Denver Botanic Gardens.

of perfection, plant a few low-growing blue *Penstemon caespitosus.*

I have a friend whose spring woodland ground cover of ferns, snowdrops and sweet-smelling violets I have always admired. In some climates one could add many of the low-growing woodland plants, such as epimedium, foamflower and ginger. These would blend with taller perennials to make a melange of ever-changing heights, shapes and textures—a moist, green, heaving sea instead of a carpet.

Out in the open and in large areas, landscape designers and architects favor the horizontal conifers because of their interesting textures and colors, and because they will grow for months at a

Themes from a Summer Place

SELECTED GRASSES

Arundo donax **'versicolor'** (striped giant reed grass) Ten feet (3m) tall, back-of-the-perennial-border selection with white striped leaves.

Hordeum jubatum (squirreltail barley) Annual grass with silky flower spikes to add motion to plantings.

Cortaderia selloana **'Sunningdale Silver'** Seven-foot (2.1-m) perennial "hotel grass" with late summer feathery panicles.

Imperata cylindrica **'Red Baron'** (Japanese blood grass) Crimson leaves are seen to best advantage with sun behind them on hills and berms.

SELECTED GROUND COVERS

Lamium maculatum (silver nettle) Pink or white flowers accent luminous creeper.

Veronica pectinata, V. filiformis Tiny blue flowers sparkle on prostrate mats spilling onto paving.

Thymus pseudolanuginosus (woolly thyme) An ideal filler for crevices and paving stones.

Epimedium X *rubrum, E. grandiflorum* (bishop's hat) Long lasting, heart-shaped leaves on wiry stems for naturalistic plantings.

Delosperma cooperi, D. nubigenum (hardy iceplant) Succulent, mat-forming leaves with bright flowers for rockeries and hot, dry situations.

BLACK GERANIUM (*GERANIUM SESSILIFORUM* 'NIGRUM') threads through the grey-blue needles of pinks and the green leaves of aster and campanula.

Chapter Seven

Silver Threads and Golden Needles

Tapestries of silver and gold,
Flowers fair and foliage bold,
Shining glints that only fade
When winter's mantle is finally laid.

Anonymous

SILVER AND GREY GARDENS

The gleam of success in this herb garden, left, comes from rose-pink *SALVIA INVOLUCRATA* 'BETHELLI', variegated SOCIETY GARLIC *(TULBAGHIA VIOLACEA)*, DONKEY TAIL SPURGE and *ARTEMISIA ABSINTHIUM* 'LAMBROOK SILVER'.

On the left overleaf, a wave of *ARTEMISIA LUDOVICIANA* 'SILVER-KING' emphasizes the pastel tones of stock, coneflower, sea lavender, liatris, lamb's ears, veronica and cupid's dart in a Denver garden. On the right overleaf, DONKEY TAIL SPURGE *(EUPHORBIA MYRSINITES)* and PARTRIDGE FEATHER *(TANACETUM DENSUM* var. *AMANI)* nuzzle together.

The English sometimes call grey gardens silver or moon gardens, evoking an image of cool refinement. Like gentlemen at the Ascot races in June, clothed in grey-striped trousers, grey morning coats, silky grey ties stuck with pearl pins and grey felt top hats, grey gardens are the epitome of debonair sophistication. Some grey-foliaged plants thrive in a lovely, cool, moist climate, where grey plants summon dreams of warmth. Most grey foliage, however, is an adaptation to the climate of more southern latitudes—the bright sunshine of the Mediterranean area, the continental territories of the United States and California. In northern maritime climates grey foliage, like grey moles and grey squirrels, is especially appealing; the soft colors blend with the greyer skies, frequent mists, and the romantically inclined garden. But with brilliant sunshine and often bitter cold winters, grey leaves are not just chic, they are a necessity. The same plants look altogether different.

Along the northern Mediterranean the bright sun shines down on fields of fragrant grey and purple lavender and orchards of gnarled grey olive trees. There the leaves of plants have evolved to cope with the sunlight and intermittent rainfall in a number of ways. Some plants are spiny or spiky, while some are narrow leafed, woolly, fat and waxy, or little leafed and low growing. Some plants have aromatic oils that may help preserve them during the cold. Many grey plants were brought to the United States so long ago that one can hardly remember which ones are natives, while others in the continental interior had already evolved in a parallel fashion thousands of years before.

My garden is on the Great Plains, called the Great American Desert by white pioneers. This part was claimed by Spain, which perhaps some

residents of New England found very appropriate. Here *Yucca glauca* grows rampant beside the interstate highways for miles, where it has uninterrupted visions of flat-topped mesas 150 miles away, antelope browsing in the early

morning, sagebrush and short grass prairie intersected with spikes of barbed wire endlessly fencing the rangeland, and spikes of other grey-green yucca throwing up rosettes of needles into a cloudless blue sky. Some years the yucca send up a

Mint green *BALLOTA PSEUDODICTAMNUS* evokes a sun-baked Mediterranean summer with *SALVIA* X *SUPERBA*, *AJUGA REPTANS* 'ATROPURPUREA' and *HELIANTHEMUM NUMMULARIUM*.

LAMIUM MACULATUM
'ALBUM', ivies, fern, ajuga
and violets, above, form a
verdant pastiche. Silver
rosettes of biennial
VERBASCUM BOMBYCIFERUM,
below, send up branching,
flowering stems fleeced with
white down during their
second year.

long, woody stem that has improbable panicles of edible, creamy green flowers. The first winter the seedpods are a dry beige color, full of shiny, black seeds large enough to be used for money. The second winter the old pods are black and stark against the snow.

There are other American yuccas, some with cream and green-striped leaves that are more exotic, but to my mind none so lovely as the wild plains natives. When gardeners grow them in maritime areas to flank elegant entrances, or to spike up their gentle landscapes, they should remember how the immigrant yucca looks at home, with hard darts silhouetted against an orange desert sunset, and white waxy bells glittering in the moonlight, attracting its only pollinator, the night-flying pronuba moth.

The agave is another sharply pointed grey foliage plant like the yucca. Agaves grow in milder portions of the southwestern United States and Mexico. Their rosette shape is so outstandingly handsome that it is worth all the trouble of potting up the plants and bringing them indoors during winter in less balmy climates. The broad fleshy leaves have a grey glaucous bloom and often pale green spines on the margins. *Agave americana* 'Variegata' has a cream stripe down the center of each leaf, further accenting its sculptural shape. Once established, agaves need hardly more attention than a plastic garden gnome and are considerably more decorative.

Much of the foliage of the native plants of the plains is grey, woolly or prickly, like the hairy little asters, senecios and artemisias. A few of the roots of true desert plants extend down as far as ninety feet. Others have a shallow, fibrous root system that extends horizontally to absorb infrequent rainfall as fast as possible.

Besides the grey, spiny plants there is a group of grey, prickly-foliaged garden plants reminiscent of thistles. Sea hollies, *Eryngium,* are grown for their silvery bracts. *Eryngium giganteum* is sometimes called Miss Willmott's ghost, and *Eryngium maritimum* is noted for bluish grey leaves with ethereal pale veins. Its flower head is surrounded by bracts that form a stiff, pale, pointed collar—like Queen Elizabeth I's lace ruff. They look their best when their upturned collars reflect the moonlight. The giant *Onopordum acanthium,* the so-called Scotch thistle, needs a lot of space in the garden. It has vast silvery grey, thistle-shaped leaves bunched in a huge rosette. The flower stems reach from six to eight feet high. One would not want to encounter this plant on a dark night but it is statuesque and astonishing. Another plant of somewhat similar size, shape and drama is the cardoon, *Cynara cardunculus.*

One more plant with grey thistly foliage is globe thistle, *Echinops ritro.* Its round flower heads have such a blue, metallic sheen that they are often mistaken for fakes. They are desirable in fresh and dried flower arrangements, and their jagged foliage makes a nice contrast growing next to a plant with rounded, waxy leaves, such as *Sedum spectabile.*

Another group of grey foliage plants has adapted to limited moisture and hot, drying sun by growing narrow leaves. Among a number of silvery evergreens, there are many junipers with handsome minute blue and grey leaves. *Juniperus scopulorum* 'Skyrocket' forms a very narrow pointed tree and is a good, dark blue-grey. It is a Rocky Mountain juniper and very hardy and drought resistant. *Juniperus virginiana* 'Burkii' is a dense, conical upright, with attractive silvery blue foliage. *Juniperus squamata* 'Meyeri' is a shrub with pendulous branches and is considered one of the most sparkling small silver trees.

Santolina chamaecyparissus, called lavender cotton, forms low, tidy mounds of silver foliage that are a very useful size and shape in the garden. It is from the Mediterranean region and has aromatic, narrow leaves. It can be left to flower, but if the hundreds of little gold daisies spoil one's color scheme they can easily be shorn off. Sometimes santolina is clipped to make miniature grey hedges to border an herb garden.

Lavenders make another compact and beautiful grey edging. Their grey leaves are well adapted to the southern European climate, where they first grew, and the fragrance of sun-warmed roses and English lavender, *Lavandula angustifolia,* is guaranteed to produce instant nostalgia and heartache in anyone who loves English country gardens. Lavenders are worth growing just for their scent, but their texture is equally alluring. Woolly lavender, *Lavandula lanata,* has the palest, grey-green leaves, while *L. pinnata* is more tender, with gorgeous feathery foliage.

One of my favorite hardy perennials with fine grey foliage is Russian sage, *Perovskia atriplicifolia.* A light, lacy-looking plant with misty blue spires of flowers late in summer, it makes a hazy, grey backdrop or delicate contrast to large-leafed grey plants like *Eryngium alpinum.*

It is hard to keep one's hands to oneself when around the woolly grey foliage. Stroking the downy leaves is a delight, and picking a few soft grey stems to plunge into a vase with pink or blue waxy blooms can make life seem worth living. One of the woolliest plants is Grecian mountain tea, *Sideritis clandestina,* a member of the mint family. An ancient and extensively used herb in the Eastern Mediterranean region, it is a splendid grey addition to a border, especially when the

pale yellow tubular flowers shine against the silvery grey leaves.

Another mint with cuddly leaves is the lamb's-ears, *Stachys byzantina,* from the Caucasus. The ears need a bit of grooming to keep them neat and furry, but they flourish in hot sun and will not rot unless allowed to get soggy.

Tall mulleins, *Verbascum thapsus,* grow wild outside my back door. In February, when the land is a monochromatic beige, finding the hoary rosettes of the biennial mullein in the sandy soil of the old, dried-up creek bed is a joy. The new elliptical leaves appear to have been cut out of apple-green velvet, and their rich relations, *Verbascum olympicum,* grow in the flower bed. They are an exciting addition to the border for their sheer size and texture. Their five-foot-tall woolly stems, covered with flowers, persist for a month or more. In summer one can almost see the flower stem growing. *Verbascum pulverulentum* and *V. bombyciferum* have vast grey leaves and yellow flowers branching out like a cathedral candelabra. With white flowers and purple centers, *V. chaixii* 'Album' would look lovely against a dark evergreen hedge, especially in the evening.

Ballota pseudodictamnus is a small, compact plant with pubescent, heart-shaped leaves. It is an unusual lime-green color with a greyish cast, and it contrasts nicely with the dark green glossy foliage of such plants as *Penstemon strictus.* A native of Crete, it thrives on neglect in brilliant sun.

Wormwood, or mugwort, is an odd name for the silvery artemisias. The native *Artemisia tridentata* and *A. ludoviciana* are the familiar sagebrush that cover millions of acres of the western United States. Many other kinds make beautiful and practical garden plants, where they will often grow in hot, dry situations, such as the

This herb garden, above, sports DWARF LAVENDER COTTON (*SANTOLINA CHAMAECYPARISSUS* 'CORSICA'). Aptly-named PARTRIDGE FEATHER (*TANACETUM DENSUM* var. *AMANI*), below, deserves a spot in any grey garden.

south side of a house. *Artemisia absinthum* 'Powis Castle' is a light and frothy plant that imparts an informal look to a bed. It has bluish grey foliage and tiny, cream-colored flowers. *Artemisia schmidtiana* 'Nana' is another tidy silver mound, perfect for the front of a border. A perennial whose foliage emerges just in time to hide the old leaves of tulips and other spring bulbs, it is so soft I have seen children stop to stroke it. *Artemisia canescens* has such fine thread-like leaves that it looks like a fichu of delicate silver lace.

The foliage of dusty miller appears to be covered with an early morning hoarfrost. Every stem, deeply divided leaf, and small round flower bud is an ocean spray turquoise-grey. This *Senecio cineraria* is merely another member of the gold-flowered, grey-leafed Compositae family, but it deserves its popularity, which it owes to elegant form and special colored foliage. These plants once adorned Victorian nosegays and now spill out of pots and flower beds with equal panache.

Some grey plants are hairless but store water in the center of their fat, waxy leaves so they can withstand periods of drought. These small plants fit into the hot, dry microclimates many gardeners have on the house's south side and may thrive in a dusty, baked corner.

In such an environment the houseleeks reign. For thousands of years sempervivum have been called houseleeks and were encouraged to grow on top of roofs because they were thought to prevent lightning from striking the house. It would be interesting to know how such wishful thinking came about, and if they ever plugged leaks in the roof or, indeed, caused them. Sempervivum and the similar echeveria grow in basal rosettes. *Sempervivum arachnoideum*, cobweb houseleek, looks as if a spider had spun white hairs

from tip to tip across the thick pointed leaves, thereby giving the plant two advantages, water storage and white hairs.

The leaves of sedums are arranged along the stem. *Oscularia deltoides* is a vigorous succulent about nine inches high, with grey oblong leaves and blush pink stems. *Sedum spectabile* is tall and mingles farther back in a flower bed, but its translucent, grey-green leaves look as if they were carved from jade and polished by a Chinese artisan. It makes a good contrast in texture to some of the feathery artemisias.

Euphorbia myrsinites flops across the front of a border, dangling elegant fronds of silver-grey leaves arranged in whorls along the stem. It is even more languid in winter, but its handsome foliage is doubly appreciated peering out from the snow, and its long grey stems can be coaxed into curves that add a lot of vitality to a flower arrangement.

Along a sunny path a number of other small, hairy and tiny or narrow-leafed plants can be woven in among the waxy ones to create splendid year-round grey, green and blue colors. These foliage textures are like a thick, hand-knitted cardigan with knobs, braids and woolly sections all blended together—and they are just as comfortable and good-looking. Most of the plants have bright little flowers on occasion, but the whole effect is worth creating for its foliage alone. Many of the plants are so attractive that gardeners grow them in pots so they can admire them more easily.

In this group is partridge feather, *Tanacetum densum* var. *amani*, which grows like a miniature fern but is a tough, small ever-grey plant. Fat round mounds of snow-in-summer, *Cerastium tomentosum*, will pour down a wall, its little white starry flowers shining against soft grey foliage. On the ground

squat pinks such as *Dianthus gratianopolitanus* 'Tiny Rubies'. This plant has tufts of narrow pointed leaves forming grey mounds that look pretty even when not sprinkled with pink flowers. The flattest and toughest rugs of grey foliage are both mountain survivors of climates far harsher than I would ever dare give them. The little grey furred leaves of pussy-toes, *Antennaria rosea,* and the rosettes of sulphur flower, *Eriogonum umbellatum* var. *subalpinum,* grow between rocks and pavings in impossibly nasty spots, and as a result should be loved and admired.

The leaves of woolly thyme are so minuscule that it could be a ground cover for a doll's house. But it will form a large mat of dark, antique grey-green foliage, accented with minute pink flowers in summer. This quintessentially hardy plant will creep up and down hot, dry stone steps and across brick patios, spreading charm wherever it goes. In winter the leaves turn a dark purplish color, akin to the neck feathers of a dove.

Grey gardens have a habit of blending with the landscape. Grey foliage echoes the tones of stone walls, tree bark and distant hills. At the same time, silvery leaves reflect sunlight and give the garden a glorious glisten.

A silver setting in the Betty Ford Alpine Gardens relies upon CERASTIUM TOMENTOSUM, newly-discovered MARRUBIUM ROTUNDIFOLIUM from Turkey, pinks, YUCCA GLAUCA, VERONICA INCANA and a background of COLORADO BLUE SPRUCE (PICEA PUNGENS).

GREY FOLIAGE AND FLOWERS

Garden flowers look especially beautiful against grey foliage. The combination of white and grey is the most obvious, but it never goes out of style. Seventeenth-century Puritan women must have been well aware of how fetching they looked in their grey dresses with white collars. Whitewashed cottages silhouetted against torn grey skies, cream pearls and grey kid gloves, grey kittens with white paws—all are cherished images. Vita Sackville-West, an eminent Englishwoman, created a famous all-white garden at Sissinghurst Castle, with an abundance of grey leaves. Fifty years later, the idea of blending smooth white, cream and green blooms with hairy or glaucous foliage is still fresh.

To create a Mediterranean look in a hot, sunny location, preferably with blue hills or ocean shimmering in the background, try planting a framework of silvery grey artemisias, santolinas, lavender, yucca and sea hollies. Then, for a white garden that will sparkle like a diamond set in platinum, one might try tiny cream tulips, *Tulipa turkestanica*, which emerge from the earth in spring like forty-carat gems. In summer these could be followed by white Asiatic lilies, such as frosty 'Mont Blanc', gleaming greenish white coneflowers, *Echinacea purpurea* 'White Swan', white irises with golden throats, and snowy gypsophila.

A host of blue and purple flowers exists for the dreamers who wish to weave lilac colors among silver foliage. Cupid's dart is a heavenly blue with a darker blue eye; *Catananche caerulea* 'Blue Giant' is a fine example. Another purplish perennial is the hardy *Aster* X *frikartii*, with forest green foliage and violet-blue daisies with yellow centers. *Penstemon strictus* has rich, dark green lanceolate leaves and flowers that offer an unbelievable combination of azure and lavender blue. (The leaves grow in pairs up the stem, typical of many penstemons.) Scabiosa bloom for weeks in the summer in soft sapphire shades. While the small shrub, blue mist spiraea, *Caryopteris* X *clandonensis*, will wait to flower until the end of summer, the sky blue is welcome in August when so many of the remaining garden and wildflowers are yellow and purple.

The most feminine garden can be created around a tender pink and dusky grey color scheme. A shrub rose such as *Rosa* X 'Pink Meidiland' looks dainty and fragile with pink petals fading to white in the center, but she is a tough lady who

The grey leaves of ARTEMISIA LUDOVICIANA 'SILVER-KING' and LAMB'S EARS *(STACHYS BYZANTINA)* form an effective showcase for the flowers of WAX BEGONIAS *(BEGONIA SEMPERFLORENS-CULTORUM),* SALVIA X SUPERBA, ANEMONE X HYBRIDA 'SEPTEMBER CHARM' and JAPANESE ASTER *(ASTERMOEA MONGOLICA).*

can deal with a Mediterranean or continental climate, as can little sea pinks, *Armeria maritima,* and several pink dianthus. For the woman with a more tempestuous nature, scarlet Asiatic lilies such as 'Firecracker' or 'Red Song' and *Penstemon barbatus,* iced down with some silver foliage, will provide a flaming red splash worthy of Scarlet O'Hara.

Helianthemum, sometimes called sun roses, will continue to flower profusely in hot sun, and their bottle green mounds of foliage contrast well with the mouse greys of dwarf achillea or snow-in-summer. A particularly pretty double, peach-colored helianthemum, *Helianthemum nummularium* 'Double Apricot', could start an unusual peach and silver garden, perhaps backed up by one of the peach daylilies, such as *Hemerocallis* 'Meadow Mist'.

Yellow and orange colors combined with grey can weave a gold and silver carpet, and they make the sunniest and most vivacious borders. One of the many candidates for this function is the brilliant orange butterfly weed, *Asclepias tuberosa,* from the same family as wild milkweed, but with brighter flowers and insignificant pods. Two popular yellow coreopsis that positively thrive in a sun-baked garden are *Coreopsis verticillata* 'Moonbeam', with clouds of daisies the color of lemon soufflé, and *Coreopsis grandiflora* 'Sunray', with double, orangey yellow flowers guaranteed to flower for weeks and provide cheer on even the most depressing days.

Silver and grey foliage does not require flowers in a single color scheme. All of these plants, and many more, can be combined to make brilliant jewel hues. With a fine and varied selection of foliage in the background, the rest is up to the gardener's wildest grey fancy.

In a German four-square garden, *opposite above,* flowers for cutting— snapdragons and *SALVIA FARINACEA*—complement the broad leaves of artichoke.

Pink globes of SEA PINK *(ARMERIA MARITIMA), opposite below,* float in front of silver *VERONICA INCANA* and its blue flower spikes.

At the Botanical Gardens at the University of British Columbia, *left,* brilliant MALTESE CROSS *(LYCHNIS CHALCEDONICA)* and BLACK-EYED SUSAN *(RUDBECKIA HIRTA)* radiate with *ARTEMISIA LUDOVICIANA* 'SILVER-KING' and GLOBE THISTLE *(ECHINOPS RITRO).*

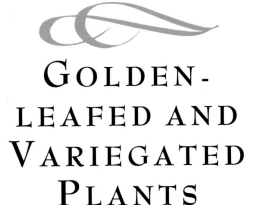

GOLDEN-LEAFED AND VARIEGATED PLANTS

Striped GARDENER'S GARTERS *(PHALARIS ARUNDINACEA* 'PICTA') are backed by yarrow and delphiniums.

The mythical King Midas wished to turn everything he touched to gold, and his reputation for greed and tastelessness is legendary. Gold foliage, however, is a glorious asset in any garden, especially when used as a highlight or to contrast blue and green leaves. Because gold-foliaged plants are often slower growing than their green-leafed counterparts, they make fine accent plants that do not outgrow their locations too quickly. There are several categories

of gold foliage: sun- and shade-loving plants, variegated leaves and all-gold foliage. While hirsute, silvery foliage is often a defense against strong sunlight, gold foliage results from a lack of chlorophyll in the leaves. Some gold and variegated foliage must stay in the shade or risk sunburn.

Some plants are golden only at certain times of the year. At the mention of golden leaves one naturally thinks of autumn, but many gold-leafed plants are gold only in spring and gradually grow greener as summer progresses. Several trees have greenish yellow leaves throughout the summer. One of the grandest is *Catalpa bignonioides* 'Aurea', a large shrub or small tree, with huge, lime-colored, heart-shaped leaves. Everything about the Indian bean tree is enormous, including the great white inflorescenses in summer.

While catalpa has elephantine foliage, the golden cut-leaf elder, *Sambucus racemosa* 'Aurea', has pinnately compound leaves, with each leaflet deeply serrated, finally terminating in a long, elegant point. It deserves its reputation as one of the most admired golden foliage plants, although the new leaves in spring emerge a pale bronze color. Close contenders for the most popular yellow tree designation are the delicately yellowish *Robinia pseudoacacia* 'Aurea' or 'Frisia', and the ancient, peculiarly leafed *Ginkgo biloba* (also known mysteriously as the maidenhair tree), a deciduous tree that turns yellower throughout the summer.

There are many conifers among the sun-loving golden plants. They not only create bright, butter-colored blocks of color in the garden but also retain their color year-round. (They could be called ever-yellows!) If planted in shade, however, they may not retain their golden glow.

Chamaecyparis lawsoniana 'Lutea' and 'Lane' are two splendid trees growing to a tall pyramid shape.

A fat little golden cone, *C. l.* 'Minima Aurea' is just right for a rock garden or small sunny space. Rumpelstiltskin may have used *Chamaecyparis pisifera* 'Filifera Aurea' when he was supposed to be spinning gold—its foliage is so fine and narrow. This small, low false cypress cascades down like golden rain, and when snow and ice cover the garden, it creates a genuine silver and gold spectacle.

Yellow junipers come in every size and shape. One practical variety, *Juniperus communis* 'Depressa Aurea', shines in the headlights of an automobile on a dark driveway at night. By day the dense, low shrub makes a yellow carpet, handsome along a grey wall or gravel path, but its foliage turns more bronze in winter.

Had King Midas studied variegated foliage, he would have realized that gilded edges are often more gorgeous than solid gold. Two lustrous examples are variegated dogwood, such as *Cornus alba* 'Elegantissima', with grey-green leaves edged in rich cream, and one of the many variegated hollies, *Ilex* X *altaclarensis* 'Golden King' (really a queen), with shiny green margins on her green leaves.

A pair of golden variegated plants that relish sun and blend with silver foliage are *Iris pallida* 'Aureo Variegata', which forms a fan of strong cream and green stripes, and *Thymus* X *citriodorus* 'Aureus'. This latter minute plant could easily be overlooked, but it bears close inspection. It has little oval green and yellow leaves that are ideal for the edge of a hot patio. Further, it is one of the finest plants for miniature flower arranging, with elegantly scaled-down twigs and branches. Variegated leaves that flaunt large splashes of gold include a striking bamboo, *Arundinaria viridistriata,* with long green pinstripes.

Dark green, palmately shaped ivy leaves have a graphic quality pictured on everything from wallpaper to wrought iron. The variegated forms are especially sought after. *Hedera colchica* 'Sulphur Heart' will dapple a shady wall with green and gold even when the sun is not shining. One of the few clear, bright yellow-leafed ivies is *Hedera helix* 'Buttercup'; it will retain its true yellow if planted in the sun. It forms a brilliant carpet or wall that gladdens the heart of the most avid gold digger.

The gold-margined leaves of *AGAVE AMERICANA* 'VARIEGATA' make a bold statement above rosettes of echeverias.

A Tapestry of Silver and Gold

SELECTED SILVER-LEAVED PLANTS

Lychnis coronaria (rose campion) Woolly rosettes contrast shocking magenta or pristine white flowers in informal beds.

Ballota pseudodictamnus Perfect to tumble down a rough wall or embankment.

Stachys byzantina **'Helene von Stein'**, **'Silver Carpet'** Edging or front of the border clumps, drifts, and bulb companions.

Artemisia absinthium **'Powis Castle'**, X **'Valerie Finnis'** Silver tracery to enhance pastel flowers and bolder foliage.

Verbascum bombyciferum (silver mullein) Impressive rosettes of grey leaves support felt-cloaked stems with yellow flowers for vertical border accent.

SELECTED GOLDEN-LEAVED AND VARIEGATED PLANTS

Symphytum X *uplandicum* **'Variegatum'** Cream-margined leaves distinguish this hybrid for the herb or perennial planting.

Humulus lupulus **'Aureus'** (yellow-leaved hop) Twining climber or border scrambler tolerant of some shade and drought.

Hakonechloa macra **'Aureola'** Green-striped yellow leaves age to sienna to pair with clumps of lamb's ears or coral bells.

Tovara virginiana **'Painter's Palette'** Green leaves are splashed with ivory, yellow and brown for mixed border.

---

*N*ICOTIANA ALATA 'NIKKI WHITE', *STACHYS BYZANTINA* and bulbous OAT GRASS (*ARRHENATHERUM ELATIUS* 'VARIEGATUM') subtly intermingle.

Chapter Eight

The Emerald Jungle

Keep a green tree in your heart
and perhaps the singing bird will come.

Chinese proverb

TROPICAL AND SUBTROPICAL FOLIAGE FOR EXOTIC TOUCHES

On the left overleaf, fiery-flowered MONTBRETIA (*CROCOSMIA X CROCOSMIIFLORA*) spark a planting with UMBRELLA LEAF (*GUNNERA MANICATA*). On the right overleaf, ANGEL'S-TRUMPETS (*DATURA X CANDIDA*, now *BRUGMANSIA X CANDIDA*), right overleaf, dangle above broad, green foliage.

It is possible to have a jungle in one's garden with none of the disadvantages of malaria and elephants trampling the foliage. The term jungle conjures up visions of enormous leaves, swinging vines, brightly colored flowers and dripping water. All these are possible in an environment far from the unpleasant heat and humidity of genuine tropical jungles. One can turn the whole garden into an equatorial paradise, but more often a small area is set aside for exotic plants. Here a lush and wild look is encouraged to evoke a mood of warmth and languor, where the gardener can recreate the feeling of the tropics, at least in summer.

It is wise to choose a location out of the wind, as many large, simple leaves are less able to withstand being desiccated than smaller, compound leaves, and they will be damaged if blown about violently. The back of a house is often a suitable place, close to a water supply. The plants in a jungle are not necessarily tropical; many may be hardy plants native to much colder climates. A tropical, wet look can be achieved easily with a combination of large, glossy leaves, feathery ferns and palm-like spikes.

To create the ambience of a jungle—a word loosely applied here to encompass any warmer, wetter environment—jungle elements must be set in place. An arbor of some kind for climbing plants to crawl over is a requisite. This could be combined with a seating area or a hammock so one can relax and look up into thick leaves and a profusion of flowers. In different parts of the country, various vines will be viable, but an exotic vine-like shrub to consider is angel's-trumpet, *Datura*, which has long, elliptical leaves and fabulous trumpet-shaped flowers dangling down enticingly. There are several hardy trumpet vines,

(*Campsis* spp.), with smaller but equally beautiful bugle blossoms in fiery colors—all of which happen to lure hummingbirds. Carolina jessamine, *Gelsemium rankinii*, has shiny evergreen leaves and can flower with a mass of yellow blooms. Persian

little waterfalls and pools where moisture-loving plants and ferns can nestle up to trail their fronds and enjoy having their leaves splashed with water. There are many small water fountains available that do not require additional plumbing; they are

*G*UNNERA MANICATA and spikes of NEW ZEALAND FLAX (*P*HORMIUM TENAX), left, are upstaged by primeval-appearing cycad palms.

*T*his patio takes on a jungle-like ambience with the addition of pots of ELEPHANT EARS (*C*OLOCASIA ESCULENTA) and BIRD-OF-PARADISE (*S*TRELITZIA REGINAE).

ivy, *Hedera colchica* 'Dentata', has large green leaves and looks tropical growing up a tree.

Water in some form needs to be present in the jungle area. It could be a pump that allows water to drip down an arbor into a trough, or a series of

merely hung on a wall or tree, and trickling water is recycled constantly with the help of electricity.

If a large pool or pond is already in place, it can be incorporated into the jungle theme with appropriately dramatic foliage and bright flowers.

The foliage can be a mixture of perennials, herbaceous plants that happen to have a more tropical air and will maintain the mood for many seasons, and a few brilliant annuals whose color and form can be altered each year to provide an ever-changing festival.

There is a group of trees and large shrubs with big simple leaves that could form the core of this area. They include several species of magnolia—stately plants with glossy, dark foliage, that have long been popular. One of the grandest, with enormous fragrant white flowers, is *Magnolia grandiflora*. Yellow-flowering *Rhododendron macabeanum* has leaves over twelve inches (30.5 cm) long, with pale, silky undersides. The foliage of the foxglove tree, *Paulownia tomentosa*, is also large enough to create deep shade, and both *Decaisnea fargesii* and *Kalopanax pictus* have a sultry tropical demeanor.

The shiny palmate leaves and elegant growth pattern of *Fatsia japonica* make it a favorite of architects, and its exotic foliage makes it an obvious choice for the emerald jungle. Even more graphic are the Chusan palms, *Trachycarpus fortunei*, with giant fans of spiked foliage waiting to be plucked by an Egyptian slave and waved over the gardener. Or try a fern as big as a tree, *Dicksonia antarctica*.

Many bamboos tolerate cold, but they summon dreams of Asiatic splendor and sunshine. *Phyllostachys viridiglaucescens* is a bamboo that will grow up to eighteen (5.5 m) feet high. It has rich, long, pointed leaves whose cool blue and green cast a refreshing pall over a hot scene.

Close to an established pond, plants that require a good deal of moisture can create a jungle scene reminiscent of Kipling's "great, green, greasy Limpopo River." *Gunnera manicata* is the ultimate in gargantuan foliage. Its leaves are big enough for the Mad Hatter's tea party, and they would make stupendous flower arrangements in a ballroom. Beside this colossus other foliage can look puny, but the strong, upright spears of *Phormium tenax* or the finely dissected compound leaves of ferns make an excellent contrast in shape, color and texture. If there is not enough room or water for the gunnera, one of the rhubarbs, such as *Rheum palmatum atrosanguineum*, would have a similar effect but with crimson coloring. The rhubarbs were originally grown in China and brought across Asia on the ancient caravan routes. Try to picture the tough camel drivers watering the red, knobby roots in their baskets of soil strapped to the heaving saddles. The wide funnel-shaped leaves of *Rodgersia tabularis* and *Petasites giganteus* and the smaller leaves of *Peltiphyllum peltatum* all look as if they should be in a Brazilian rainforest but will flourish thousands of miles farther north.

Dark, bronzed foliage can increase the sensation of heat and torpor in a garden. Castor bean, *Ricinus communis* 'Gibsonii', has all the attributes associated with a jungle. It is fast growing, has immense palmate leaves, heavily veined with a leathery texture and sheen, and it has unusual dark red leaves and seedpods.

To complete the look of luxuriant greenness, an emerald carpet of foliage is needed. *Euonymus fortunei* and ginger, *Asarum europaeum*, with heart-shaped, wet-looking leaves, are both examples of temperate climate ground covers that would tolerate the heavy shade of large-leafed plants and would, with only a little imagination, appear suitably torrid.

Jungle foliage requires exotic blooms and hues. Many gardeners prefer the brilliant, hot colors of central American fabrics—a weaving of scarlets,

fuschias, oranges and purples—to carry through the ambience of gaiety and panache. Six-foot (1.8-m)-tall annual cannas, with butterfly blooms and wide plastic-like foliage, are the perfect complement to tropical-looking leaves. With a collection of hanging baskets drooling the fulsome blossoms of tuberous begonias, and big containers of tender banana trees, *Musa basjoo,* and rubber plants, *Ficus elastica,* one can create a setting worthy of an Amazon queen.

<u>Jungle Gems</u>

Phormium tenax **'Purpureum'** (New Zealand flax) Dark, spiky clumps for vertical accents.

Ricinus communis (castor bean) Quick-growing African annual to ten feet (3m) or more for bold statement.

Gunnera manicata (umbrella plant) Waterside magnificence in deep, organically rich soil.

Rheum palmatum **'Atrosanguineum'** (red ornamental rhubarb) Large, deeply cut leaves topped by early summer crimson flower panicles for perennial border.

Musa basjoo (banana) If proper winter housing is available, nothing can top the tropical flavor of bananas summering outdoors.

Bananas triumph at Wave Hill in late summer, towering over cannas, iris and blue fescue grass.

Chapter Nine

Domestic Bliss

I have often thought that if heaven had given me a choice of my position and calling, it should have been on a rich spot on earth, well watered, and near a good market for the productions of the garden. No occupation is so delightful to me as the culture of the earth, and no culture comparable to that of the garden.

Thomas Jefferson, 1743–1826
in a letter to Charles Wilson Peale

HERB, KNOT AND EDIBLE GARDENS

This lakefront garden in Montana, right, combines the textures of sunflowers, calendula and dill.

On the left overleaf, potted standards of rosemary, ivy topiary and CHENILLE PLANT (*ACALYPHA HISPIDA*), grace a formal square at Meadowbrook Farm. On the right overleaf, the view of the Palisades above the Hudson River at Wave Hill is framed by a collection of foliage plants, including hosta, croton and flowering maple with creeping zinnia.

It is possible to have a beautiful garden where only useful plants are grown, either to eat, flavor food or provide fragrance or dried material around the house. As gardens get smaller, and the time available to spend in them grows shorter, this makes a good deal of sense. Practical gardens have been cultivated for well over two thousand years, and they still are in many parts of the world where growing plants merely for beauty may be considered an unseemly luxury. Many gardeners find it satisfying to return to these ancient cultural values, and the smaller the garden, the more practical they seem.

Herb gardens have been planted in northern Europe since medieval times, when hundreds of plants were cultivated for medicinal uses, dyes, fragrance, food flavoring, and simply to eat. Following the practices of the Greek and Roman empires, the monasteries planted walled herb gardens where cherished plants, including those from the Mediterranean area, were cared for and harvested. In those days, growing the plants and learning how to use the different parts was a matter of survival. Banks' Florilegium, published in 1525, said of the herb rosemary, "if thou be feeble boyle the leaves in clene water and wash thyself and thou shalt wax shiny." Would that it were so easy today. Now entering a separate, formal herb garden is like travelling back in time. It engenders a feeling of tranquillity that we associate, perhaps falsely, with more serene and simple times.

There are many ways to plant an herb garden. Geometrically designed beds, edged with low hedging, can be planted purely for visual pleasure, with plenty of attractively shaped plants, or for color and foliage texture, provided by plants such as prettily flowering sweet false chamomile, *Matricaria recutita*, and bright green parsley, *Petroselinum crispum*. The same garden can be filled with herbs selected for their fragrance, such as lavender and sweet woodruff; or stuffed with

sixteenth-century patterns, and are kept carefully manicured to maintain the design. The spaces between are filled with colored pebbles or more small herbs.

The traditional hedgings of box, which appear

potherbs for the kitchen such as thymes, tarragon and mints. Or a collection of herbs from all over the world can be assembled. To make an Elizabethan knot garden, rows of low-growing herbs are planted in interweaving ribbons, following

almost black in the shade, provide precise, graphic outlines for some of the more loosely growing and wayward herbs. For a more Mediterranean mood, as well as pale grey colors, lavender cotton, *Santolina chamaecyparissus*, lavender, *Lavandula angustifolia*, and rosemary, *Rosemarinus officinalis*, can be clipped into tidy little hedges. One can even edge herb beds with more herbs. Chives, *Allium schoenoprasum*, and thrift, *Armeria maritima*, both make a tussocky edging just a few inches high, and bloom with spheres of tiny pink flowers. Old-fashioned plants that look charming with a mature herb garden include columbine, iris, hollyhock, flax, feverfew and, of course, old roses.

Partly owing to a lack of space for a separate herb garden, partly to fashion and partly to a new willingness to be adventurous in the garden and kitchen, herbs are being grown everywhere. They can be found in pots, window boxes and hanging baskets, in raised beds and mixed among other perennials and annuals in borders.

Several herbs that are too tall for the low knot garden have traditionally been placed elsewhere. Herbs such as fennel, *Foeniculum vulgare*, which has misty clouds of foliage rather like asparagus fern, can be useful in a flower border. Fennel combines well with the biennial herb angelica, *Angelica archangelica*, which makes a stronger, green statement. Borage is an annual worth growing if only for its star-shaped, bright blue flowers that can be floated enticingly in summer drinks. It is also a handsome, easy-to-grow plant, with woolly, grey-green simple leaves, and it self-seeds readily. Borage, however, tends to flop over, and it would benefit from being placed between stout-stemmed perennials such as gay-feather, *Liatris*, and coneflower, *Echinacea*.

Clary sage, *Salvia sclarea*, is one of the stars of any border. Coarse, hairy leaves contrast with delicate-looking, pinkish bracts enclosing minuscule flowers. The bracts glow when the sun shines through them, and, like many bracts, they last for weeks. Some herbs, such as the spearmint *Mentha*

spicata, are so robust and even invasive that they can be relegated to a strip of soil by the garage or back door or grown in containers. Sunflowers, *Helianthus annuus,* are favorites, although their height and great, hairy stems and foliage are rather uncompromising, making them hard to situate in a garden. They are a natural in the golden Midwest of America where their size is echoed by the vast expanses of blue sky and rolling plains. Sunflowers look splendid in a prairie garden paired with blazing Indian blanket flower or fireweed, *Gaillardia* X *grandiflora,* and shining yellow coreopsis. They are also spectacular in a city garden on a grey rooftop, where their bulk and huge, tawny heads are not intimidated by surrounding buildings. Sunflowers are another essential in a practical garden, because their seeds can be eaten or given to the birds.

Herbs are not the only useful plants that can be incorporated successfully into the garden. James Woodforde, an English country parson who was always short of money, wrote in his diary on June 11, 1788: "We had a very excellent Dinner, that is to say, a fine Piece of fresh Salmon with Tench and Eel, boiled Ham and Fowls, the best part of a rump of Beef stewed, Carrots and Peas, a fore Qr. of Lamb rosted, Cucumbers and Mint Sauce, a Couple of Ducks rosted, plain and Currant Puddings. After Dinner 2 large Dishes of Strawberries, some Blanched Almonds with Raisins and Aples." With the possible exception of the raisins, everything came from his farm and garden or the river close by; and until the turn of this century this was not unusual. A separate walled kitchen garden with rows of leafy vegetables and herbs, rhubarb bulging under inverted pots and a raspberry cage full of canes protected from the birds can be great joy.

Edible landscapes can be created in any small garden as long as there is enough sun—as most vegetables and herbs will not produce satisfactorily under trees or in shade from buildings. The scarlet flowers of some pole beans can decorate an arbor or veranda supports, where the dangling seedpods look almost tropical under the profusion of foliage. Cucumbers, melons, squash, pumpkins and gourds are all fast-growing annuals with large foliage that will provide deep shade by August if trained up a strong trellis. Peas and tomatoes and nasturtiums for salads can be trained vertically in tight spaces, and their foliage is decorative while one waits for the harvest.

Peppers and eggplants are pretty enough to be planted in formal borders and can be decorative in informal gardens with their simple leaves and colorful waxy fruit. The fruit of purple eggplants looks handsome among the airy blossoms of lilac-colored sea lavender, *Limonium latifolium,* where the big leathery leaves mimic the eggplant's shape. Vivid green lettuce makes a frilly border, or several lettuce plants can be grouped together to provide a contrast in texture to herbs such as chives. The dark green crinkly leaves of chard and spinach are best shown to advantage in raised beds. Even if chard is not a favorite vegetable, it is worth growing for flower arranging and to see the early morning sun shining through its beautiful, wine red petioles and main veins. The lacy rosettes of ornamental kale adorn many flower beds; the green and white ones make a fine accent in a sea of flowers, while the fat, florid shapes look oddly luxurious spilling out of pots with similarly colored annuals. Some of the scented herbs are tender, and the pots can be brought inside to a sunny window where a crushed leaf will remind one of a redolent summer.

A pastoral setting enhances a pretty patch of corn, pumpkins and flowers for cutting.

Red-stemmed Swiss chard (*Beta vulgaris* 'Ruby Chard') is usually relegated to the vegetable garden, but is striking in the flower border.

MAKING AN ENTRANCE

A tidy gardener might pick up the fallen crabapples and miss how they complement a planting of polka-dot plant, begonia, dracaena, dusty miller, coleus, vinca and lobelia.

Of all the people who visit one's house, only a favored few will be invited in to enjoy the relaxing areas of a back terrace or patio, and only a few dear friends will take an interest in the rest of the garden. It is important, then, to decorate the front of the house with year-round foliage. Shrubs and vines can cover part of the masonry, thorny plants can discourage intruders and pots of plants can be massed at the door to greet guests.

The fashion for covering buildings with foliage has fluctuated from one extreme to the other over the past hundred years. Virginia creeper, *Parthenocissus quinquefolia,* and Boston ivy, *Parthenocissus tricuspidata,* have been softening the façades of the world's colleges and public buildings for centuries. In England some Victorians with a back-to-nature zeal allowed ivy to overgrow buildings so completely that only indistinct green mounds were visible. Other architects and designers stripped the same buildings bare to show respect for their craft. But few houses are so distinctive that they cannot be improved by the addition of flowers and foliage lodging against their walls.

Although Victorian postcards of robins singing on windowsills edged with spring blossoms seem hopelessly idyllic these days, birds will sing and nest against a house if there are plants growing up the walls. Attractive shrubs that will grow against a house include some of the buddleia, such as *Buddleia globosa,* and yellow-blooming pineapple broom *Cytisus battandieri.* Mexican orange, *Choisya ternata,* is an evergreen shrub with engaging glossy leaves and sprays of white waxy flowers. The early spring blossoms of flowering quince, *Chaenomeles,* are

always enchanting. Its gnarled branching habit and small leaves, so often depicted in Chinese paintings, look especially beautiful against grey stone. There is also something appealing about magnolias, such as *Magnolia stellata,* leaning against the brick walls of a house. Their thick evergreen leaves give a home a substantial and permanent appearance, and the blossoms, which look like white tulips, are a bonus.

The most romantic decorations for a house have to be the classic roses. From the many choices there are climbers such as 'New Dawn', which will grow twelve to fifteen feet (3.7–4.6 m) high and wave soft, pink, fragrant flowers outside a bedroom window; or 'Albertine', with peach-colored blooms that can be picked from a kitchen casement. On the north side of a house, climbing ivy is a natural. Varieties such as the variegated, yellow-leafed *Hedera helix* 'Gold Heart' provide an illusion of dappled sunshine where none exists, and the dark green leaves of an ivy such as *H. h.* 'Baltica' make a fine design clinging to white clapboard.

Shrubs can loiter casually against a house in a countrified manner. Creepers can be trained tidily up a wall, and their leaves, which overlap like fish scales, can appear quite manicured. The most unnatural, and hence most architectural use of foliage, is espaliered trees, which can be cunningly trained to echo the structure of the house and frame windows or doors.

On the shady side of a house, shrubs of espaliered pyracantha, such as *Pyracantha coccinea,* make sense. It has little white flowers, red berries, small neat evergreen leaves and sharp thorns to deter all but the most determined trespassers. It is also easy to grow in poor soils and can be trained readily along wires or a

A flow of *CLEMATIS MONTANA* 'RUBENS' effectively drapes a fountain, even out of bloom.

trellis. Growing tall enough to reach the second story of a house, *P. atalantiodes* makes a handsome, formal evergreen decoration.

In milder climates, common fig, *Ficus carica*, will amble casually up a house or against a wall, its glossy foliage contrasting stunningly with a stuccoed surface. In the brilliant sunshine and warmth of southern California and Florida, an array of subtropical shrubs and vines thrives, but most impressive on those dazzling whitewashed walls is the bougainvillea, whose bright blossoms and pillowy sprays of foliage spill over the walls with enviable exuberance.

Beside a front door, containers of restrained and formal evergreens can be maintained to provide a sophisticated and aloof entryway. Standard bay or box trees, clipped to a geometric shape and placed on either side of a front door are a time-honored decoration, and they send a traditional don't-call-me-I'll-call-you message. The same message can be conveyed by an asymmetrical grouping of pruned and potted junipers or containers of agave, green and white coleus and sempervivums. Pots of blooming lilies and pelargoniums can be added on days when visitors are welcome.

The back terrace, however, should have a completely different mood, with flowers and foliage immediately outside the windows to provide an ever-changing view. Louis XIV of France, the Sun King, started a fashion at Versailles for planting orange trees in vast pots that were wheeled onto terraces in summer and back indoors into orangeries in winter. Today tropical and subtropical plants are readily available to bring outside each summer to create an oasis of luxuriant green foliage, or to mix with more

A basket of variegated treasures holds impatiens, lamiastrum, abutilon, ground ivy, FUCHSIA X 'GARTENMEISTER BONSTEDT', browallia and marigolds.

temperate annuals in pots for bursts of color.

To enhance the architecture of a grand house, fine urns can be sited with mathematical precision on a terrace. They can be placed in rows or arcs to form a perspective, and used as pointers to lead to other parts of the garden. Large containers can be used as accents. The Victorians were fond of installing elaborate urns in the center of their circular flower beds, where lofty plants added height and color to their carpet bedding schemes. In other types of gardens, pots can be placed in niches or put on a pedestal as the focal point at the end of a walkway.

In cottage and more informal gardens, pots can be bunched together in friendly groups on patios or around garden seats and ponds to provide movable feasts of color and diversity. Troughs of aromatic herbs such as apple mints and scented-leaf geraniums can be placed at strategic points to waft delightful fragrances over visitors. Pots of vines can be heaved high onto walls to trail their foliage down lengths of brick or stone. In towns and cities, pots and window boxes of spring bulbs, summer foliage and bright flowers can be displayed against sooty stonework and clinging balconies. There is no end to the creative possibilities with container gardening. The following are just a few ideas for using good foliage in pots.

Containers of bamboo seem to work particularly well with contemporary architecture. Tall golden goddess bamboo, *Bambusa glaucescens*, and dwarf white-striped bamboo, *Arundinaria variegata*, are good examples. Many bamboos are so invasive that some gardeners will grow them only in a confined space; imprisoning

them in an elegant great pot is an ideal solution. When designing containers of mixed plants, the foliage and color scheme should be planned first and the flowering plants added later. Large formal pots on terraces look splendid with rosettes of spiked dracena at the center, surrounded by lots of flowers, and a profusion of foliage such as vinca trailing over the edges.

Some of the tropical and subtropical plants that will thrive on northern sunny terraces and patios during the summer are croton, *Codiaeum,* from Asia, with large, brightly colored leaves, and elephant's-ear, *Colocasia,* a member of the lily family with heart-shaped leaves up to two feet (61 cm) across. Calla lilies can often be persuaded to bloom in pots on patios. Some species have large, arrow-shaped leaves with silver speckles and long arching petioles, wonderful for flower arranging. The polka-dot plant, *Hypoestes phyllostachya,* is another good choice, with dark green leaves spattered with pink, white or crimson freckles that can be echoed in the blooms of matching flowers. Chinese basil, *Perilla frutescens,* is a purple member of the Coleus family with a fine metallic sheen, particularly useful when placed with blue and pink flowers. The white and lime green varieties of caladiums, such as *Caladium candidum,* create invigorating patterns, flourish on shady patios and look spectacular massed with other greenery such as lotus vine and asparagus ferns.

Sprays of linear foliage in containers always have a cooling effect in hot situations. Bulbs of Peruvian daffodils, *Hymenocallis,* can be grown in pots indoors, then taken outside in summer. They have straplike leaves and wonderfully bizarre white flowers. The lovely Abyssinian gladioli, *Acidanthera,* also have sword-shaped foliage and look their best when a dozen or

more are grown in a large pot.

Lilies are perhaps the loveliest summer container bulbs. Unlike many plants they enjoy being baked in the sun in clay pots and will cope for several days without watering. Even when they have finished flowering, their shiny whorls of leaves are an asset. The most exquisite may be the climbing lilies, *Gloriosa rothschildiana,* which flourish on warm patios placed beneath a trellis, where they clamber up and bloom with elegant red and yellow flowers whose great recurved petals look like the flames emerging from a rocket. They are a great investment; for the price of a few bulbs one can feel as rich as the Rothschilds, dining beside a cascade of lilies.

Magnolia grandiflora, left, presides over a seasonal display of ivy, lamiastrum and impatiens.

Vinca and impatiens, above, make an understated windowbox planting.

Ivy, below, joins the minimalist movement.

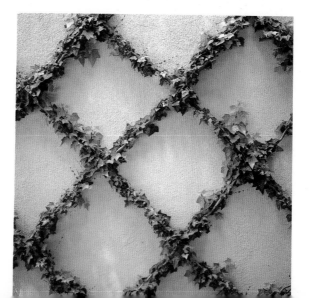

Household Hints

SELECTED HERBS AND VEGETABLES

Pelargonium spp. (scented geraniums) Varied in aroma and shape and pretty in herb groupings or pots.

Hibiscus esculentus (Abelmoschus esculentus) (okra) Handsome, divided leaves on tall plants with purple-eyed yellow flowers pretty enough for the flower border.

Angelica archangelica (angelica) Deeply divided leaves topped by umbels of chartreuse flowers.

Salvia officinalis **'Tricolor'**, **'Purpurea'** Selected varieties of common sage valuable for color in herb plantings.

Ocimum basilicum **'Purple Ruffles'** (purple basil) Excellent contrast for grey-leaved herbs.

SELECTED CONTAINER PLANTS

Abutilon pictum **'Thompsonii'** (flowering maple) "Rice paddy" leaf markings make it a standout specimen.

Acalypha wilkesiana (copperleaf) A bold plant to combine with nemesia or begonias.

Helichrysum petiolaire **'Limelight'** Could not be prettier than with ivy geraniums.

Hypoestes phyllostachya (polka-dot plant) Pink, red or white "freckles" on deep green leaves make it a good mixer with other shade annuals.

Lotus berthelotii (parrot's-beak) A waterfall of silvery foliage for mixed pots or hanging basket.

The finely cut leaves of DILL *(ANETHUM GRAVEOLENS)* grace a garden in Montana.

Chapter Ten

The Garden Composed

And I beseech you, forget not to inform
yourself diligantly as may be, in things that
belong to gardening.

John Evelyn, 1620–1705

PERFECT PARTNERS

On the left overleaf, pastels dominate a composition, with *LIATRIS PYCNOSTACHYA* 'FLORISTAN WHITE' as the dominant element, supported by oriental lilies, *PRUNELLA X WEBBIANA* 'PINK LOVELINESS', *NICOTIANA ALATA* 'NIKKI WHITE', shasta daisies and *ARTEMISIA LUDOVICIANA* 'SILVER-KING'. On the right overleaf, imagine the fragrance on a warm afternoon walk through ENGLISH LAVENDER (*LAVANDULA ANGUSTIFOLIA*) at Hidcote Manor Garden.

Most gardeners will find it rewarding to spin a globe and make a note of those places in the world—in both hemispheres—where latitude, altitude and distance from an ocean are similar to his or her own area. These places can then be researched to find out if there are new and interesting additions that can be made to the garden. For example, the land masses that correspond closest to Denver, Colorado—which has a latitude of forty degrees, an altitude of five thousand feet (1500m) and is about one thousand miles (8045km) from an ocean—are central Turkey, the foothills of the Pamirs, part of China west of Beijing and bits of Patagonia. Some unusual plants from these particular areas flourish at the Denver Botanic Gardens and are gradually becoming more available to gardeners there. Finding such a partner for one's plants from the other side of the world is both a delight and a surprise to the garden visitor.

While many plants have crossed the continents for hundreds of years, there are still some handsome specimens that are not widely known outside their areas because they lack economic value of some kind. Gardeners looking merely for beauty, however, have created a whole new market for plants, some of which have been cultivated for centuries, and others that have been disregarded. One caveat—take care that wild and rare plants do not become depleted from their native habitats.

Once the gardener's geographic niche has been pinpointed, and local features such as soil type and the attitude of the land toward or away from the sun have been determined, the fun starts. The quest is to find plants that are an exact match, then persuade them to take root in one's garden.

Recently ordinary American acorns were collected for an arboretum in Hungary. What is regarded as a weed in Afghanistan or South Africa may become a treasure in Zurich or Atlanta. If it is appealing and not poisonous or illegal, grow it, and disregard the opinions of the rest of the world as to its merits.

Plant partners can also be found closer to home.

The chartreuse form of FEVERFEW
(*CHRYSANTHEMUM PARTHENIUM* 'AUREUM')
finds a garden mate with *LAMIASTRUM*
GALEOBDOLON 'HERMAN'S PRIDE'.

Creating different combinations of two or three
plants is an endless source of fascination to
gardeners. Take for instance, one of the pasque
flowers, *Pulsatilla vulgaris,* which is at its best in
spring when its very hairy sprays of deeply divided
foliage spout forth, encircling equally hairy tulip-
shaped flowers. The leaf and flower color are too
similar to grow next to the hellebores, such as
Helleborus purpurascens, although they do bloom at
the same time. But the pasque flower looks even
more purplish and downy tucked in next to the stiff
little daggers of yellow *Iris danfordiae,* or the waxy
branches of *Euphorbia myrsinites* with its knots of
bright lime flowers.

Partnerships can be more subtle than direct
contrasts. Blending green-and-white-speckled
foliage with sharp stripes and solid greens can be
as handsome as the mix-and-match fabrics and
wallpapers that are so fashionable today. Choosing
to have the foliage of one plant echo its partner is
a touching theme that sends little thrills of
recognition up and down a gardener's spine.

COMPOSING A
GARDEN WITH
FOLIAGE AND
FLOWERS

The sylvan setting of this garden is an effective place for *HELICHRYSUM PETIOLAIRE* 'LIMELIGHT' amidst the greys and greens of *DRACAENA MARGINATA* and *ARTEMISIA LUDOVICIANA*.

Purple blooms of LAMB'S EARS, WHITE FEVERFEW and scarlet MALTESE CROSS are striking against the mountains.

Planning a garden is like composing music. It is not enough to jot down an abstract collection of beautiful notes. They should be put together in lyrical phrases, then harmonious movements, and finally, linked in a grand symphony. Think of the groups of plant partners as the phrases, the flower borders and major groupings as the movements, and the whole property, of whatever size, as the symphony. It may not take quite as much work and creativity to make a well-turned garden as it does to compose a symphony, but it can be as absorbing and the results as diverse as a contemporary composition, an eighteenth-century masterpiece, or a rhapsody of pastoral airs.

Foliage can play many roles in the garden. Beautiful as they are, flowers are but fleeting design elements in an herbaceous border. Even the most carefully orchestrated combination of plants will have moments of silence. During the winter the foliage can carry the tune for months. Tall, silvery grasses, like giant eulalia, *Miscanthus sinensis* 'Sarabande', arching gracefully over the back of the border, can provide a cadence of music throughout the year, which can be echoed with other soft mounds of evergreen foliage. This plant and many more can add a distinctive rhythm to a border. They can be filled in with a mass of flowering perennials and annuals, depending on the gardener's design predilection.

Sooner or later one must choose a theme for the garden, even if it is an accidental one—perhaps provided by a previous owner—a natural feature or a man-made structure. Once selected, this theme can be carried throughout the garden to turn it into a unified whole. In large gardens there may be room for several themes, but these can be united by design devices, such as hedges of similar foliage, or walkways edged with coordinating foliage plants, to provide a recognizable melody repeated through the property.

Simply selecting a single foliage plant, such as a traditional box, can link all the elements of a garden together. Or a simple color scheme, such as variegated green and white foliage mixed with solid green, can provide unity between a front and back garden, and set backdrops for a blaze of blinding color. Grey foliage provides a variation on a theme in a bright, sun-filled garden, while dainty foliage can set the right beat in a small-scale garden or a limited space.

Foliage can also set the tone of one's garden. Slick, glossy, smooth-margined foliage imparts a modern and urban attitude. Alternatively, soft, hairy rosettes of leaves, or plants with a floppy, relaxed mound—such as lamiums, campanulas, and nepetas—convey the feeling of cottage gardens and rural estates.

There are literally thousands of plants available for the garden, but a successful combination need only include a few special trees and shrubs, some ancient herbs, a number of favorite old perennials and some of the latest and exciting new hybrids. Every day, more hybrids are being created to accentuate interesting leaf colors and shapes. Some hybrids are also spawning smaller and more compact plants that fit into today's smaller gardens.

As our world population doubles in the next generation, it is going to become more important to be able to grow lavish green foliage in tight spaces, in tubs and on roof tops. It may become a necessity to make a small oasis of tranquility, so that one can have at least a passing acquaintance with nature. Even if one cannot see the stars at night because of urban glare, the street lights can still gleam on the glossy foliage of one's camellias.

Heuchera micrantha 'Palace Purple' adds drama to a combination of JASMINE TOBACCO *(Nicotiana alata)*, HOUND'S TONGUE *(Cynoglossum amabile)* and *Ageratum* 'Cut Wonder'.

Sources

The following fine mail-order nurseries and seed merchants offer a diverse selection of foliage plants in the United States. This list is by no means complete.

APPALACHIAN GARDENS
Box 82
Waynesboro, PA 17268
(717) 762-4312
Unusual trees and shrubs
Catalogue, Free

BAMBOO SORCERY
666 Wagnon Road
Sebastopol, CA 95472
(707) 823-5866
Wide range of bamboos
Catalogue, $2.00

KURT BLUEMEL, INC.
2740 Greene Lane
Baldwin, MD 21013
(301) 557-7229
Ornamental grasses, aquatics, ferns, perennials, bamboos
Catalogue, $2.00

BLUESTONE PERENNIALS
7211 Middle Ridge Road
Madison, OH 44057
(800) 852-5243
Sedums, ground covers, many perennials
Catalogue, Free

BOEHLKE'S WOODLAND GARDENS
W. 140 North 10829
Country Aire Road
Germantown, WI 53022
(215) 674-4900
Native plants for northern gardens
Catalogue, $0.50

W. ATLEE BURPEE COMPANY
300 Park Avenue
Warminster, PA 18991
(215) 674-4900
Comprehensive plants and supplies
Catalogue, Free

BUSSE GARDENS
Route 2, Box 238
Cokato, MN 55321
(612) 286-2654
Many hardy perennials
Catalogue, $2.00 (deductible)

CACTUS BY MUELLER
10411 Rosedale Highway
Bakersfield, CA 93312
(805) 589-2674
Cactic and succulents
Catalogue, $2.00

CAMELLIA FOREST NURSERY
P.O. Box 291
125 Carolina Forest
Chapel Hill, NC 27516
(919) 967-5529
Camellias and conifers
Catalogue, $1.00

CANYON CREEK NURSERY
3527 Dry Creek Road
Oroville, CA 95965
(916) 533-2166
Uncommon perennials, dryland and silver-leaved plants
Catalogue, $1.00

COLVOS CREEK NURSERY
1931 Second Avenue #215
Seattle, WA 98101
(206) 441-1509
Trees and shrubs
Catalogue, $2.00

CARROLL GARDENS
P.O. Box 310
444 East Main Street
Westminster, MD 21157
(800) 638-6334
Perennials, herbs, woodland plants, roses
Catalogue, $2.00

COMPANION PLANTS
7247 N. Coolville Ridge Road
Athens, OH 45701
(614) 592-4643
Ornamentals, woodlands
Catalogue, $2.00

CLIFFORD'S PERENNIAL & VINE
Route 2, Box 320
East Troy, WI 53120
(414) 968-4040
Cottage garden perennials and vines
Catalogue, $1.00

COLORADO ALPINES, INC.
P.O. Box 2708
Avon, CO 81620
(303) 949-6464
Alpine and rock gardens
Catalogue, $1.00

THE COOK'S GARDEN
Box 65
Londonderry, VT 05148
(802) 824-3400
Extensive vegetables and salad greens, heirloom seeds
Catalogue, $1.00

COOPER'S GARDEN
2345 Decatur Avenue North
Golden Valley, MI 55427
(612) 591-0495
Daylilies, hostas, iris
Catalogue, two first-class stamps

CROWNSVILLE NURSERY
P.O. Box 79
Crownsville, MD 21032
(301) 923-2212
Perennials, grasses, herbs, ferns
Catalogue, $2.00 (deductible)

FOLIAGE GARDENS
2003 128th Avenue S.E.
Bellevue, WA 98005
(206) 747-2998
Extensive ferns
Catalogue, $2.00

FORESTFARM
990 Tatherow Road
Williams, OR 97544
(503) 846-6963
Western native perennials and woodlands
Catalogue, $3.00

FOX HILL FARM
Box 7
Parma, MI 49269
(517) 531-3179
Extensive herbs
Catalogue, $2.00

GARDEN PERENNIALS
Route 1
Wayne, NE 68787
(402) 375-3615
Perennials and daylilies
Catalogue, $1.00

GIRARD NURSERIES
Box 428
Geneva, OH 44041
(216) 466-2881
Flowering trees and shrubs
Catalogue, Free

GOODWIN CREEK GARDENS
Box 83
Williams, OR 97544
(503) 846-7357
Perennials, herbs, wildflowers
Catalogue, $1.00

GRIGSBY CACTUS GARDENS
2326 Bella Vista Drive
Vista, CA 92084
(619) 727-1323
Cacti and succulents
Catalogue, $2.00

HASTINGS, H.G., CO.
Box 4274
Atlanta, GA 30302
(800) 334-1771
Southeast garden specialists
Catalogue, Free

HOLBROOK FARM AND NURSERY
P.O. Box 368
Fletcher, NC 28732
(704) 891-7790
Mixed perennials, natives, woodland heaths, heathers
Catalogue, Free

M. & J. KRISTICK
155 Mockingbird Road
Wellsville, PA 17365
(717) 292-2962
Conifers and Japanese maples
Catalogue, Free

LAMB NURSERIES
East 101 Sharp Avenue
Spokane, WA 99202
(509) 328-7956
Perennials, alpines
Catalogue, $1.00

LOGEE'S GREENHOUSES
55 North Street
Danielson, CT 06239
(203) 774-8038
Tropicals, exotics, begonias
Catalogue, $3.00

MILAEGER'S GARDENS
4838 Douglas Avenue
Racine, WI 53402
(414) 639-2371
Extensive perennials
Catalogue, $1.00

MONTROSE NURSERY
P.O. Box 957
Hillsborough, NC 27278
(919) 732-7787
Cyclamen, primula, rock garden, perennials
Catalogue, $2.00

NICHE GARDENS
1111 Dawson Road
Chapel Hill, NC 27516
(919) 967-0078
Southeastern natives, grasses, herbs, perennials
Catalogue, $3.00

PARK SEED CO.
Cokesbury Road
Greenwood, SC 29647
(803) 223-7333
Comprehensive selection
Catalogue, Free

PLANTS OF THE SOUTHWEST
930 Baca Street
Santa Fe, NM 87501
(505) 471-2212
Drought-tolerant plants
Catalogue, $1.50

PRAIRIE NURSERY
P.O. Box 365
Westfield, WI 53964
(608) 296-3679
Prairie plants, grasses, seeds
Catalogue, $3.00

RICE CREEK GARDENS
1315 66th Avenue N.E.
Minneapolis, MN 55432
(612) 754-8090
Alpine and rock gardens
Catalogue, $2.00

ROCKY MOUNTAIN RARE PLANTS
P.O. Box 200483
Denver, CO 80220
Rock and alpine seeds
Catalogue, $1.00 (Nov. only)

SHADY OAKS NURSERY
1000 19th Avenue N.E.
Naseca, MN 56093
(507) 835-5033
Shade plants
Catalogue, Free

SISKIYOU RARE PLANT NURSERY
2825 Cummings Road
Medford, OR 97501
(503) 722-6846
Alpine and rock gardens
Catalogue, $2.00

SUNNYBROOK FARMS HOMESTEAD
9448 Mayfield Road
Chesterland, OH 44026
(216) 729-7232
Perennials, hostas, ivies, herbs
Catalogue, $1.00

TALAVAYA SEEDS
Route 2, Box 2
36A Tesuque Drive
Espanola, NM 87532
(505) 753-5801
Native vegetable seeds
Catalogue, $1.00

TAYLOR'S HERB GARDENS
535 Lone Oak Road
Vista, CA 92084
(619) 727-3485
Herb plants and seeds
Catalogue, $3.00

THOMPSON & MORGAN, INC.
P.O. Box 1308
Jackson, NJ 08527
(908) 363-2225
Comprehensive seed selection
Catalogue, Free

WAYSIDE GARDENS
Garden Lane
Hodges, SC 29653
(800) 845-1124
Wide selection of woodlands and perennials
Catalogue, $1.00

WE-DU NURSERIES
Route 5, Box 724
Marion, NC 28752
(704) 738-8300
Rock gardens and woodlands
Catalogue, $1.00

WELL-SWEEP HERB FARM
317 Mt. Bethel Road
Port Murray, NJ 07865
(908) 852-5390
Perennials and herbs
Catalogue, $2.00

WHITE FLOWER FARM
Route 63
Litchfield, CT 06759
(203) 567-0801
Comprehensive selection
Catalogue, $5.00

Bibliography

Baron, Robert C. *The Garden and Farm Books of Thomas Jefferson*. Golden, CO: Fulcrum, 1987.

Billington, Jill. *Architectural Foliage*. Great Britain: Ward Lock Limited, 1991.

Bloom, Adrian. *Conifers for Your Garden*. New York: Charles Scribner's Sons, 1972.

Capon, Brian. *Botany for Gardeners*. Portland, OR: Timber Press, 1990.

Chatto, Beth. *The Green Tapestry*. New York: Simon & Schuster, 1989.

Coombes, Allen J. *Dictionary of Plant Names*. Portland, OR: Timber Press, Inc., 1985.

De Bray, Lys. *The Green Garden*. Topsfield, MA: Salem House Publishers, 1988.

Elliott, Brent. *Victorian Gardens*. Portland, OR: Timber Press, 1986.

Everard, Barbara and Morely, Brian. *Wild Flowers of the World*. New York: Avenel Books, 1988.

Flint, Harrison L. "The Year-Round Hedge." *Horticulture* (December 1985) 30–37.

Flint, Harrison L. "The Four-Season Hedge." *Horticulture* (August 1985) 26–33.

Forsell, Mary. *Heirloom Herbs*. New York: Villard Books, 1990.

Glattstein, Judy. *Garden Design with Foliage*. Pownal, VT: Garden Way Publishing, 1991.

Griswold, Mac. *The Golden Age of American Gardens*. New York: Harry N. Abrams, Inc., 1991.

Grounds, Roger. *The Multi-Coloured Garden*. London: Palham Books Ltd., 1982.

Hill, Thomas. *The Gardener's Labyrinth*. Oxford, England: Oxford University Press, 1987.

Kelly, John. *Foliage in Your Garden*. New York: Penguin Books, 1988.

Lightfoot, Mary. "Planning A Silver Garden." *The Herb Companion* (December 1991/January 1992) 52–56.

Lloyd, Christopher. *Foliage Plants*. New York: Random House, 1973.

Overy, Angela. "A Walled Garden." *Fine Gardening* (January/February 1991) 69–73.

Poor, Janet M. *Plants That Merit Attention*. Portland, OR: Timber Press, 1984. The Garden Club of America.

Preston, Richard J. *Rocky Mountain Trees*. New York: Dover Publications, Inc., 1968.

Proctor, Rob. *Annuals*. New York: Harper Collins, 1991.

Proctor, Rob. *Country Flowers*. New York: Harper Collins, 1991.

Proctor, Rob. *Perennials*. New York: Harper Collins, 1990.

Quinn, Vernon. *Leaves*. New York: Frederick A. Stokes Company, 1937.

Sanecki, Kay N. *The Book of Herbs*. Leicester, England: Magna Books, 1988.

Spencer, Roger. *Growing Silver, Grey & Blue Foliage Plants*. Kenthurst, Australia: Kangaroo Press, 1987.

Springer, Lauren B. "Large-Leaved and Silver-Leaved Perennials and Their Use in Design." Thesis, Pennsylvania State University, 1989.

Steffey, Jane. "The Barberry Family." *American Horticulturist* (April 1985) 4–9.

Stephenson, Ashley. *The Garden Planner*. New York: St. Martin's Press, 1981.

Thomas, Graham Stuart. *Perennial Garden Plants*. London: J.M. Dent and Sons, Ltd., 1976.

Thomas, Graham Stuart. *Plants for Ground-Cover*. Portland, OR: Sagapress, Inc./Timber Press, Inc., 1990.

Thompson, Robert. *The Gardener's Assistant*. London: Blackie & Son, 1859.

Verey, Rosemary. *The Art of Planting*. Boston: Little, Brown and Company, 1990.

Woodforde, James. *The Diary of a Country Parson 1758–1802*. Oxford: Oxford University Press, 1978 (passages selected and edited by John Beresford).

Woods, Christopher. *Encyclopedia of Perennials; A Gardener's Guide*. New York: Facts on File, 1992.

ACKNOWLEDGMENTS

Rob Proctor's brilliant talents as
an author, artist and photographer are appreciated
by an ever-increasing circle of admirers.
It is a joy and privilege to work with him.

We extend our thanks to the generous gardeners whose beautiful foliage and flowers
appear in the photographs on the following pages, including:

Kurt Bluemel *(p. 3)*
Chanticleer Garden *(pp. 30, 36, 44, 131)*
Sally Cole *(pp. 78-79, 112)*
Charles Cresson *(p. 142)*
Fran Davies *(p. 143)*
Clari Davis *(p. 50)*
Martha Davis and Rich Sayrs
   (pp. 88-89)
Denver Botanic Gardens *(pp. 16, 17, 23, 28–29,
   32, 40–41, 45, 53, 65, 80, 82, 87, 90, 91,
   94–95, 97, 98–99, 103)*
Betty Ford Alpine Gardens *(pp. 37, 42, 105,
   107, 110))*
Angela Foster *(p. 59)*
Pam Frost *(pp. 24, 77, 121)*
Hidcote Manor Garden *(p. 139)*
Lorraine Higby *(pp. 100, 114–115, 138)*

And our special thanks to:

Ray Daugherty ▪ Douglas County Extension Office ▪ Helen Fritch ▪
Betsy Gullan ▪ Ruth and Frank Harold ▪ Josephine Hopkins ▪
Tweet Kimball ▪ Corinne Levy and Tom Segal ▪
David Macke ▪ Patty McDonough ▪ Peta Poore ▪ Jack Potter ▪
Sally McLagan ▪ Suzanne Shephard ▪ Susan Sheridan ▪ Linda Staley ▪
David Tarrant ▪ Becky Thomas ▪ Joe Tomocik ▪ Caroline Writer

We are also grateful for the invaluable expertise of
Solange Gignac, of the Helen Fowler Library, Denver Botanic
Gardens, Panayoti Kelaidis and Lauren Springer.

Lainie Jackson *(pp. 56–57)*
Linda Johnson *(p. 127)*
Steve Kiely and Mike Gonser
    (pp. 33, 72–73)
Ruth Koch *(p. 130)*
Ladew Topiary Gardens *(pp. 60, 66, 70–71,*
    84–85)
Kathy Leishman *(p. 76)*
Laurie McBride *(pp. 62–63)*
Meadow Brook Farm,
    J. Liddon Pennock, Jr. *(pp. 49, 58, 124, 134)*
Laura Meissenburg *(p. 74)*
Bill and Joy Miller *(pp. 46–47)*
New York Botanical Gardens *(pp. 48, 82, 93)*
Pennsylvania Horticultural Society *(p. 69, 104)*
The People's Light and Theater Company
    Perennial Garden *(p. 108)*
Joanna Reed *(pp. 43, 51, 86, 102)*
Pamme Reed *(pp. 136–137)*
Scott Arboretum, Swarthmore College *(p. 27)*
Lauren Springer *(pp. 110, 141, 144)*
Sheila Stephens *(pp. 104–105)*
Strybing Arboretum *(pp. 96, 116, 118)*
Bea Taplin *(pp. 128, 135)*
University of British Columbia Botanic
    Gardens *(pp. 111, 117)*
Van Dusen Gardens *(pp. 12, 13, 113, 133)*
Wave Hill, Marco Polo Stufano *(pp. 25, 38,*
    61, 92, 122–123, 125)
Christopher Woods *(p. 119)*